Andrew Watson

The World's First Black Football Superstar

D1637583

Tony Talburt

H
HANSIB

First published in 2017 by Hansib Publications Limited
P.O. Box 226, Hertford, SG14 3WY
United Kingdom

info@hansibpublications.com
www.hansibpublications.com

ISBN 978-1-910553-62-6

A CIP catalogue record for this book is available from the British Library

Produced by Hansib Publications Limited

ACKNOWLEDGEMENTS

The writing of this book would not have been possible without the involvement of a number of key individuals to whom I am greatly indebted. To begin with, I am tremendously grateful to Richard McBrearty of the Scottish Football Museum in Glasgow, for being so helpful in providing a number of key materials on Watson's involvements in Queen's Park Football Club and Scottish football more generally. In addition, Richard was extremely helpful in providing information through our numerous telephone conversations and our personal meeting in Glasgow, as we tried to visit some of the actual places where Watson lived and played football while he was in the city. I would also like to express my thanks to the staff at the Scottish Football Museum for granting me permission to reproduce photographs from their archives of Andrew Watson.

I must also say thanks to Dr David Alston not only for introducing me to his website on Highland Scots and their involvement in the Caribbean in the eighteenth and nineteenth centuries, but also his two essays on Scottish Highlands peoples in Guyana. These were very useful in providing background information about Scottish involvements in Guyana, especially during the mid-nineteenth century. My thanks are also due to the staff of 'Kick It Out' for their general support and encouragement during the writing of this book. In this regard, I am extremely thankful to Lord Herman Ouseley for recognising the significance of this book on Andrew Watson, and agreeing to write a foreword in appreciation of Watson's contribution to British football. Once again, Arif Ali and the team at Hansib Publications were more than just publishers. They have been partners in the writing of this book, and were very supportive of this project, especially with Watson being a fellow Guyanese.

ABOUT THE AUTHOR

Tony Talburt graduated from the University of the West Indies (Mona, Jamaica) with a B.A. in History and Social Science (1987). He completed an M.A. in International Studies from the University of Warwick (1990) and his PhD at the South Bank University in London (2001). Dr Talburt's main research interest is in the areas of international development and African and Caribbean politics and history. His publications include: *Food of the Plantation Slaves of Jamaica* (2004), *Rum, Rivalry and Resistance: Fighting for the Caribbean* (2010) as well as the ground-breaking children's novel *History on the Page: Adventures in Black British History* (2012). He lectures in the Centre for African and International Studies at the University of Cape Coast in Ghana.

CONTENTS

LIST OF ILLUSTRATIONS

PREFACE

There have been many studies done and books written on the subject of Football. After all, this is the world's most popular sport. A few of these books have examined the contributions of key footballers past and present. None of these, however, have examined the contributions of the Guyanese-born footballer named Andrew Watson. The book begins by considering why it is that, despite his outstanding achievements and personal contributions to the development of football in the 1870s and 1880s, his name has been virtually erased from our national memory.

Watson was the first Black player to win three national cup winners trophy. He was the world's first Black person to work as a football club administrator. Watson was the first Black person to be selected for the British elite and exclusive amateur football club called Corinthians. He was the world's first Black person to captain a national team when he captained Scotland in 1881 in a match against England. He also appeared to have invested some of his personal wealth into the development of the Parkgrove Football Club in Glasgow in the 1870s. In addition to the above, he was, by all accounts, one of Britain's best defenders. This book, therefore, discusses Watson's main achievements in, as well as is contributions to, the early development, modernisation and, ultimately the 'export' of this particular brand of football to the rest of Britain.

Above all, this book argues that even though other prominent Black sports people were often unable to realise their full potential as a result of the racial discrimination they experienced, especially during the second half of the nineteenth century, Andrew Watson was able to rise above such negativity and accomplish tremendous success. Nowhere else is this better demonstrated, than in his selection for the Corinthians Football Club. His very inclusion in this team indicates the extent to which he was accepted as a member of the British social elite. For a Black person to achieve such levels of social acceptance and respect was something which was not very common in Victorian British society. This is, therefore, the first book to examine the life of Andrew Watson as Britain's first Black football superstar and pioneer of the modern game.

FOREWORD

I share a similar heritage to Andrew Watson, having been born in Guyana myself, so his story is an intriguing one on many levels for me, and one which ultimately deserves more recognition and to be told to future generations.

I have no doubt this book will do just that and illustrate Andrew's achievements in greater detail.

How he travelled to Britain to finish his education at that time is a story in itself, but for Andrew to then play football to an incredibly high standard at amateur club level, and internationally for Scotland, featuring in some magnificent results for his nation which, quite possibly, would result in national holidays were they to happen today, is something truly unheralded in the modern game.

Football in its contemporary form is unrecognisable to the game it was in the nineteenth century, however you just hope that those involved in the game are there for their love of the sport, like Andrew was.

As you'll no doubt read in these pages, Andrew Watson was a remarkable footballer, as the Scottish Football Association's Annual of 1880/81 acknowledged, but his impact was greater than his skill on a football pitch.

There have been many pioneering footballers over the years, including a number of prominent Black players who have made a considerable impact on the game, despite suffering terrible discrimination, but Andrew was a shining light of the amateur game.

Perhaps the sheer number of years since his time has meant he has been forgotten by some, but his impact can still be seen and felt. The every move of a modern player is covered step-by-step in great detail. This shouldn't let us forget the achievements of Andrew and the many who have followed in his footsteps.

For me, aside from his abilities on the pitch, the fact he was club secretary at Queen's Park and Parkgrove FC in Glasgow speaks volumes. More than a century on we are still campaigning for further diversity within football clubs and associations, thus underpinning his reputation as a true trailblazer for the game.

For his talent to be displayed at Queen's Park, a powerhouse of a club in those days, and for a team whose motto means 'to play for the sake of playing' seems even more appropriate. While the game continues to evolve, the enjoyment, beauty and unique nature of the sport shouldn't be forgotten.

Lord Herman Ouseley
Chair, Kick It Out
March 2016

CHAPTER ONE

Background and Introduction

This book about Andrew Watson, the Guyanese-born football superstar (1856-1921), is not only needed, but seriously overdue. My first interest in writing about Andrew Watson goes back to the winter of 2010. At that time I was working on a children's Black British history story-book of short fictitious accounts based on Black people who lived and worked in Britain *(History on the Page: Adventures in Black British History,* 2012). My aim in that book was to write fictionalised stories about Black people in Britain as a way of addressing the dearth of material on Black British history stories suitable for children. Some of the characters in the book included; Septimius Severus, the African Emperor who once ruled Britain, William Davidson, the Jamaican-born revolutionary involved in a daring plot to overthrow the British Government in 1820, and also the Trinidad-born Claudia Jones, a Pan-Africanist and Marxist who was regarded as the founder of the Notting Hill Carnivals in London. Although, as a life-long Tottenham Hotspur football supporter, I initially intended to include Walter Tull in this children's book as an example of an outstanding Black sports person in Britain, in the end, that never happened.

I wrote a short fictionalised story based on the main achievements of Andrew Watson. Since then, I have not looked back, and the more I have read about Watson, the more convinced I became that I had made the right decision to include him in that initial work. However, Andrew Watson's story deserves more attention than a few pages in a children's Black British history story-book, as important as that work is. Since 2010, therefore, I have had a desire to write a book specifically dedicated to highlighting the significance of Andrew Watson, Britain's first Black celebrity football superstar and pioneer.

Perhaps some may question the use of the term superstar to describe a footballer like Watson, but I believe this is a most fitting impression, given the vast array of personal qualities and outstanding achievements he accomplished both on and off the field. In Peter Seddon's book about *Steve Bloomer, Football's First Superstar*, (1999) he makes a most convincing and compelling case demonstrating how Bloomer was Derby County Football Club's first big superstar. There are two interesting points which arose from Seddon's book which resonated with my own experiences while working on this publication about Andrew Watson's contributions to the modern game of football. Firstly, in Seddon's work, it was popularly assumed and understood, especially by Derby Country supporters and football historians generally, that Kevin Hector was the club's first superstar. After all, he had scored two hundred and one goals for the club. Secondly, despite the outstanding achievements of Steve Bloomer, very few people seemed to have remembered his history and contributions to the club. As it turned out, Steve Bloomer played five hundred and twenty five times for Derby and scored three hundred and thirty two goals for the club, thus making him a greater goal scorer than Hector (Seddon, 1999, p. 9). All too often, however, the writers of history can seemingly suffer from amnesia and virtually overlook very significant individuals and contributors to the subject they are studying.

The question Seddon puzzled over was, why had Steve Bloomer been either forgotten or his achievements not fully appreciated? In similar vein, it has to be asked, why so many people (some of whom are discussed below) have assumed that Arthur Wharton and Walter Tull were the two earliest Black football pioneers in Britain. Secondly, it was important to know how or why it is that we know so little about Watson. In Seddon's work, notwithstanding these set-backs and lack of general knowledge about Derby County's forgotten hero, he went on to show how, as far as he was concerned, that Bloomer was the club's first football superstar because of his outstanding achievements and also because he was the first player to accomplish so much for the club. In this regard, Seddon's argument is valid. If this is true for Bloomer, then what this book attempts to do, is to justify that such a claim is equally applicable to Andrew Watson, who, as this work demonstrates, must surely be regarded as the world's first Black football superstar and pioneer during the period of the 1870s and 1880s.

Had Watson been playing football one hundred years later, in the 1980s, for two of the very best teams in the world, he would most certainly have been considered a sporting celebrity. For, as is demonstrated in chapter four of this book, Watson not only played for three of the world's top football teams, but was the captain of the Scottish national football team in 1881 as well as club secretary of his local team, Queen's Park in the mid-1880s. Both these teams were the very best in Britain during that decade. What he achieved in the 1880s was probably the equivalent of contemporary legends such as Lionel Messi of Barcelona or Cristiano Ronaldo of Real Madrid captaining both club and country. In more ways than one, Andrew Watson was truly a remarkable footballer and sporting hero.

According to Andrews and Jackson (2001) the sporting celebrity was a person who combined elements of a hero as a result of having gained popularity arising from their achievements, as well as stars who cultivated public interests in their own personifications (Andrews and Jackson, 2001, p. 2). Part of the problem with this study is, of course, the fact that the era of the modern sport celebrity really began in earnest with William Randolph's Hearst's establishment of the first newspaper sport section within the *New York Journal* in 1895 (Andrews and Jackson, 2001, p.6). Therefore, before the 1890s, the idea of sporting celebrity was not really known or appreciated.

It is a pity that popular sports stars and heroes did not really begin to appear on the scene until the early twentieth century, otherwise the likes of Watson would have certainly been regarded as a sporting superstar. Instead, what we have, by way of great sporting celebrity names, are people like W. C. Grace, the West Country doctor who was born in 1848 and played cricket until he was in his fifties in the early 1900s. Another popular sporting celebrity was C.B. Fry, a cricketer, footballer and athlete, who was captain of both the cricket and football teams at Oxford and played cricket for surrey in 1891 and also went on tour to South Africa in 1895-96. He was also very keenly involved in other sporting activities such as hunting, shooting and fishing (Lowerson, 1995, pp. 70, 71).

Given this state of affairs, it is hardly surprising that outstanding players like Watson, who played for three of the top teams in the world during the 1880s would be virtually forgotten within a generation. However, there are other considerations which need to be taken into account in order to help explain why Watson's name and contributions to the development of the modern game of football, have not received considerably more attention. It is against this background that two of the reasons or justifications, as well as the overall significance of this present study are discussed.

First and foremost, the Caribbean region is not usually associated with global football superstars, so a study on Watson is important in filling a gap in terms of the significance of the Caribbean in this regard. This is not to suggest that the region has not produced sporting greats. The Anglophone Caribbean, for example, has fashioned some sporting legends over the years. In the sport of cricket, one could mention Sir Garfield Sobers and Brian Lara as examples of superstars. Similarly, the Jamaica athletes Arthur Wint, Herb Mckenley and, more recently, Usain Bolt certainly stand out as extraordinary international sportsmen. In terms of international netball, some of the Anglophone Caribbean nations such as Barbados and Jamaica are highly rated. With regard to international football, however, the Caribbean region has not had the same level of success. A part from Dwight York of Trinidad and Tobago, who played for Manchester United at a period when they were considered one of the very best club teams in the world, the Caribbean region is not noted for its ability to produce many footballers of high international standards, whose name readily stands out amongst the very best in the world.

The second reason why this book is important is because it seeks to examine the significance of Watson not only as a great Guyanese-born, Black British footballer, but also as part of the wave of players who contributed to the very development of the modern game of football in England at its most crucial period in history towards the end of the nineteenth century. In this sense, therefore, the book asserts that Watson was a Black football pioneer. He actually played a part in the very development of the modern game of football as we know it today, as it emerged in the late nineteenth century from Scotland and the north of England to the rest of the country. In addition, the book seeks to redress the overall prevailing state of affairs in which Andrew Watson's name and achievements have become relatively unknown and forgotten.

The organisation of the book

Following this introductory chapter, the second chapter builds on the successes of Watson and considers why he, along with so many other sporting celebrities during the Victorian period, and even more recently, especially in Britain, have been discriminated against, or largely ignored, unrecognised and unappreciated. This chapter also looks at the level of racial discrimination which some outstanding Black sports people experienced. The main purpose of chapter three is to provide a biographical overview of the life of Andrew Watson with particular reference to his football career. The emphasis, therefore, is to focus on his journey from his birth place in Guyana to the height of his career as a footballer in the 1880s. This chapter also provides a brief political, economic and social overview of life in Guyana generally and the region of the Demerara River specifically, in the second half of the nineteenth century where Andrew Watson's family was from. Secondly, this chapter examines the significance of links between Caribbean expatriates and their off-springs in Britain and especially in Scotland where Watson's father was from, and where he himself lived and played football for most of his career. This is significant as it helps to set the scene and provide the overall background and context of Watson's life and his subsequent achievements as a player, as well as his social standing in this Victorian period of British history. What is important here is the extent to which these two different geographical areas of the world were closely related through important colonial trade and commercial ties.

The main purpose of the fourth chapter is to examine Watson's achievements with two of the main Scottish football teams he played for, namely, Queen's Park Football Club in Glasgow and the Scottish national football team. This is very important, as in effect, Watson played for three of the very best teams in the world at that time, which helps to demonstrate the reason for his rise to fame within Scotland and subsequently, in England as well, due to his remarkable football accomplishments. The chapter begins by providing an overview of the origin and development of the modern game of football in Britain, before focusing its attention more specifically, on the situation in Scotland where Watson began his football career. The significance of this stems from the fact that the development of the game more broadly, is important in helping to contextualise the significance of Watson's role as a football pioneer, with regard to the general emergence of the particular nature of football which would come to be played in England.

Chapter five explores this theme of the development of football further, by looking at the influence of Scottish players and personnel upon the game in England in the critical period from the 1870s and 1880s. It begins by exploring the significance of the decade of the 1870s through to the end of the century when the nature, rules and style of football were being developed, and then focuses on the role of the 'Scottish professors' during this period in the development of the modern game of football in England. The third aim of the chapter is to examine the importance of Watson as one, among hundreds of 'Scottish professors' who came to England, and effectively introduced the combination style of football associated with passing and dribbling which was not emphasised in England.

The main purpose of the sixth chapter is to examine the significance of social elitism in football and Watson's role within this, especially with regard to his involvement with the Corinthians Football Club. The London-based Corinthians Football Club was the most elitist football team in Britain in the 1880s and 1890s. The chapter makes the point that Watson was very privileged and was certainly able to mix very well with some of the elite figures involved in development of football at this time. Much of the focus, therefore, is on Watson's life as a fairly wealthy and educated Black man at this period of British history and his contributions to the development of the game. Chapter seven provides a summary and also considers the reasons why Watson's name and legacy should not be forgotten, whether this is with reference to Britain or the country of his birth, Guyana.

CHAPTER TWO

Rediscovery, Recognition and Reminiscence of Black Sporting Success

This chapter begins by discussing the extent to which outstanding Black sporting personalities have been forgotten or virtually removed from our national consciousness. This is, of course, examined with particular reference to Andrew Watson. The key concern in this regard, is the reason why more of our sports historians, writers and British society in general, have failed to recognise and celebrate the extraordinary achievements of outstanding Black sporting icons to a much greater extent. Secondly, although Andrew Watson's playing career does not appear to have been over shadowed by racial discrimination, other notable Black footballers, performing during this period, were certainly not spared from such discriminatory taunts and practices. In this regard, a few brief examples are highlighted to show the extent to which the lives of some outstanding Black sports people were adversely affected.

In his interesting column in the *National Sport* (2010), Robert Philip remarked that he had no way of knowing whether Andrew Watson was as great a player as legend suggested. Part of the reason why Philip felt this way was probably because, despite Watson's remarkable achievements both on and off the field, not a great deal had been written about him, thus resulting in his name being removed from the national consciousness. Interestingly enough, Philip correctly acknowledged that Watson was the world's first Black international footballer. This alone would make a study on Andrew Watson a worthwhile undertaking. However, he did much more. He was the world's first Black football administrator as he worked as the secretary at two different football clubs in Scotland. The first was Parkgrove FC in the 1870s and then for Queen's Park in the

1880s. He was also the world's first Black footballer to play in a FA Cup final in England. Therefore, as has already been noted, Watson's football qualities were so good that he was also privileged to play for three of the very best teams in the world in the 1880s, namely, Queen's Park, the Scottish national team and also the very elite amateur club, Corinthians of London. He was the first Black footballer who could be singled out as part of the wave of Scottish pioneers, who helped to introduce a new style and approach to the game of football into England, and ultimately the rest of the world. Watson's crowning act, however, must surely be the fact that he captained the Scottish national team which beat England 6-1 in 1881 at the Kennington Oval in London. This still remains England's heaviest defeat on home soil. He was thus the world's first Black footballer to captain a national team when he captained Scotland. Robert Philip virtually answered his own question, by citing a contemporary newspaper which declared that 'Andrew Watson could be considered among the finest players in the whole of Britain' (Philip, 2010). In this very short report by Philip, which is interestingly entitled 'a hero and a football pioneer,' he certainly does not conceal his overall enthusiasm and support for Watson. So, despite Philip's initial doubt in his question, the article paints a picture of Watson as both hero and pioneer. In both respects, these descriptions are perfect in their overall characterisation of Watson. He was more than just a good Black footballer.

In addition to Watson's football abilities, he was also a qualified engineer and travelled extensively to America and Australia and, because of his relative financial security and education, could be considered as a member of the social elite within Britain. As will be discussed later in this book, it was his level of education and privileged background, which also ensured that he was able to have been selected to join the very exclusive and elite amateur football club in London, called Corinthians.

That Andrew Watson was a greatly respected footballer and a gentleman can hardly be in doubt. In the *Scottish Athletic Journal* of 15 December 1885, they presented a glowing portrayal of Watson which certainly makes this point. In the article entitled 'modern athletic celebrities,' Watson was singled out for his remarkable achievements, which included his prize in the high jump competition, in which he jumped five feet ten inches at the Queen's Park Sports Competition in 1879. This was not a one-off situation, as he was reported to have won forty awards in high jump competitions. He also competed in boat races on the River Thames while at school in London. Although standing at six feet and weighing about thirteen stones, he was reported to prefer to play the ball, rather than charge his opponents, which the newspaper article thought was something other players ought to have copied. He was also subjected to vulgar insults by ill-tempered players, yet he preserved a gentlemanly demeanour which endeared him to supporters and team-mates a like.

Part of what makes this present work important, is the fact that it suggests that Watson not only played football at the highest level during the 1880s, but was doing so at the time when the very nature of some aspects of the game were being radically transformed, developed and, ultimately exported to England and the wider world. Moreover, it was during this period that Scotland (where Watson played most of his football) was able to transfer their particular 'passing' style of football to England. That Andrew Watson, who was very definitely an integral part of this Scottish approach, should be either ignored or forgotten is a travesty and, makes it necessary at the very least, that his story be told, remembered and recognised as one of the pioneers during this very early phase in the development of the modern game of football in Britain. Even though a more thorough biographical overview of Watson is provided in chapter three, from this very brief summary of his main achievements provided above, it is still puzzling that Watson's story has not received much more emphasis in a number of important studies on the origin and development of the modern game of football in Britain.

Whilst the presence of Black football players in post-war Britain is fairly common-place in the modern game, very little has been written about their involvement prior to this period.

Even where there have been academic books on Black footballers in Britain before the Second World War, Andrew Watson's name is rarely mentioned. The few studies which have concentrated on Black footballers have tended to focus on the names Arthur Wharton who was born in Ghana in 1865 and Walter Tull who was born in Kent, England in 1888. It is these two names which are mentioned as the two earliest Black footballers in Britain. In fact, recent tributes and commemorations have quite rightly been held in Britain to remember the achievements of Arthur Wharton and Walter Tull, but very little has been done to mark the accomplishments of Andrew Watson in Britain or in his homeland of Guyana in the Caribbean.

In fact, it seems strange to think of a world-class footballer coming from the Caribbean. However, Ferguson (2006) notes that by the end of the nineteenth and early twentieth century, the game of football had not only been introduced into the Caribbean, but that several players from the region had made significant contributions in world football by the second half of the twentieth century in the sense that many of them left to play in Europe for some of the top clubs. (Ferguson, 2006, pp. 32, 33). These included players like Clyde Best, Jamaican-born John Barnes, Thierry Henry from Guadeloupe and Edgar Davids who was born in Suriname and later played for Holland. In this sense, therefore, a few Caribbean-born footballers have been influencing world football for several decades. It would, however, be wrong to assume that this wave of Caribbean, or Black players participating in the English football league was a more recent experience. Hinds (2006) would, in his work called *Black Lions,* acknowledge that Andrew Watson should be rightly acknowledged as the first great Black soccer player (Hinds, 2006). Similarly, Ferguson's work on the significance of African and Caribbean footballers also makes some reference to Andrew Watson. These two publications at least, made mention of the significance of Caribbean footballers to the world game. More recently, an international Caribbean conference on Caribbean football was held at the University of the West Indies, Mona, Campus in Kingston, Jamaica in April 2014. One of the aims of this conference was to explore the nature of the state of football in the region within the context of the globalised nature of the game. Resulting from this conference, the first academic book on Caribbean football was published in 2015 (Charles, 2015). From this, it is clear that the influence of African and Caribbean players on the globalisation of football in recent times has been significant.

In addition to this work by Charles, Ferguson had also written an earlier account of the influence of Caribbean players on football in the region as well as on a global scale. He recounts how, in the 1950 FIFA World Cup Competition, England suffered a shock defeat 1-0 to the United States of America. Whilst this was certainly a shock, what was even more surprising was the fact that the goal-scorer of the America winning goal was a Caribbean–born footballer who had 'qualified' to play for the USA, whose name was Joseph Edouard Gaetjens (Ferguson, 2006, pp. 14, 15). Gaetjens was born in Port-au-Prince, Haiti in 1924 to a Haitian mother and a Belgian father. Gaetjens had been born into a fairly wealthy family and eventually became a member of the US national squad and returned to Haiti as a hero. However, it is believed that some of his relatives may have been critics of the authoritarian regime in Haiti. In 1957, Francois 'Papa Doc' Duvalier had been elected president, but his regime was based on a programme of consolidating power by force, with the help of his own private and personal militia to target rivals. Many people in Haiti who dared to challenge his authority would be forcefully eliminated through torture and death. It is widely believed that Gaetjens was mysteriously taken away by military forces and was presumed to be dead as he was never seen again. The general point, however, is that a few footballers from the Caribbean were able to make their presence felt on the international scene.

Although these Caribbean-born players have been singled out for mention, they were all part of the post war period and, it is often assumed that Black people had little impact on the game prior to this period. Of course, this point is further strengthened by the fact that it was after the Second World War that Caribbean teams started to make their presence felt within the FIFA world Cup Competition. For instance, Haiti played in the World Cup in 1974, while Jamaica qualified in 1998 and Trinidad and Tobago achieved a similar feat in 2006.

Where studies have recognised the significance of Black players in Britain, Andrew Watson's contributions have received little or no attention. This example is clearly seen in Vasili's very important work (1998) on Arthur Wharton. He makes the point most powerfully, that Wharton was Britain's first Black professional footballer in the late 1880s. In this respect, he is correct, as Wharton played at the time when the professional game was in its infancy. Watson was playing from the middle of the 1870s until the late 1880s before the professional era. What is very interesting about Vasili's study is the fact that a number of other notable White footballers born outside Britain, who played at the national level, were also highlighted. For example, James Frederick Mcleod Prinsep, who was born in India, was singled out for special mention. He not only played for Clapham Rovers in the 1870s, but also had one national cap for England against Scotland in 1879, and was regarded as the youngest player to play for England at the age of 17 (Vasili, 1998, p. 74). He also mentions two non-White players who played at the national level. The first was Eddie Parris of Bradford who was selected by Wales in 1931 and was the first Black player for their national team. The first non-White player for England was Hong Y 'Frank' Soo who played in 1941 (Vasili, 1998, p. 76).

In Vasili's later work on the history of Black footballers in Britain, it is very clear in its position that Arthur Wharton was a unique Victorian sports star (Vasili, 2000, p. 17). During his twenty years in competitive football, this saw him play for a number of clubs including; Darlington, Rotherham Town and Preston North End (Vasili, 2000, p. 19). Once again, a number of Black footballers who played football professionally in the immediate years following the First World War were singled out for special mention. For example, an Egyptian, Tewfik Abdullah signed for Derby County in 1920. Another Black player named Jack Leslie made three hundred and eighty two appearances for Plymouth Argyle in the 1920s (Garland and Rowe, 2001, p. 34). Hamilton and Hinds (1999) similarly made the point that among the names of Black footballers who paved the way for later generations, were Arthur Wharton and Walter Tull (Hamilton and Hinds, 1999, p. 8). They, very importantly, mention the significance of other players such as Albert Johanneson and Steve Mokone as examples of Black footballers who played in England in the late 1950s and 1960s (Hamilton and Hinds, 1999, p. 9). The key point to note is that Andrew Watson is not mentioned at all, even though, as argued in this current book, he was certainly equal to some of the aforementioned Black players in terms of footballing achievements, and could even be regarded to have achieved more, by virtue of playing for the very best teams of his day.

More generally, where studies have examined the origin or development of football in Britain in the late nineteenth century, the same kind of pattern can be observed where Watson's name was not mentioned. For example, Lowndes (1952) mentioned some of the great players of the English game. Among the players singled out for special attention were; Steve Bloomer of Derby, Billy Meredith of Manchester City and Peter Doherty of Blackpool and then Manchester City (Lowndes, 1952, pp. 93-100). Similarly, in Golesworthy's *Encyclopaedia of Association Football,* (1973) under the heading of 'Coloured Players' he, like Vasili, noted that Parris who played for Bradford, Luton Town, Northampton Town, Bournemouth and Boscombe Athletic between 1928-1939, was the only 'coloured' player to appear in an international championship (Golesworthy, 1973). In like manner, Tim Hill's *Encyclopaedia of World Football* (2008) has a chapter devoted to the 'legends of football' to which the name Andrew Watson does not appear. In a separate chapter on 'great clubs' there is also no mention of the Corinthians Football Club which, from the period in the 1880s until the first World War, was certainly one of the best club teams (albeit an amateur team) in Britain.

Even the very important work by Robinson (1920) on the history of Queen's Park Football Club, which actually mentions the names of team members, does not provide detailed commentary on any individual. For example, he discusses how and when the team was formed in 1867, as well as their main achievements during the first fifty years of their existence. As the different teams and officials during that fifty year period were mentioned, it becomes clear who played for the team and in what year. Only very brief commentaries or annotations were provided about some of the individual players. It was within this context, too, that Watson's name was mentioned as one of the players in the victorious Queen's Park side which had won the Scottish Cup and the Glasgow Charity Cup in the season 1880-1881. In a couple of places (discussed below), Robinson commented on Watson's actual playing ability. In general, however, detailed discussions about footballers, especially outside of England prior to the 1890s, were few and far between.

This series of omissions or amnesia could also be seen in another context. This has to do with a significant international football match between England and Scotland on 12 March 1881 in London at the Kennington Oval. This match was significant for at least two reasons. Firstly, England lost 6-1 to Scotland, thus making it their heaviest ever defeat on home soil. Secondly, the captain of this victorious Scottish team, and arguably, one of the best footballers in the country at the time, was a Black man named Andrew Watson. Not only has Watson's name been forgotten, but even this very game has hardly been written about.

Discussions about outstanding Scottish games against England seem to mention two popular matches which occurred in the twentieth century. The most recent of these was the game which was played in 1967 when Denis law's goal ensured Scotland beat England 2-3 at Wembley Stadium in London. This game was also famous for the football antics of Jim Baxter who famously teased the England players with his skills by playing keepie-uppie down the wing. This game, coming just one year after England had won the World Cup, led many of the Scots to regard themselves as the unofficial world champions. The second game which is also singled out for mention between England and Scotland, was the one played in 1928. In this game Scotland beat England 5-1 and were described as the Wembley Wizards. It is worth noting, as an example of this, that Lowndes regarded this as a standout international match between England and Scotland when, a very good Scotland team, completely outplayed England and beat them 5-1 (Lowndes, 1952, pp. 54, 55).

Of course, another famous match occurred where England exacted their revenge by solidly beating Scotland on 15 April 1961 by a very high-scoring 9-3. The general point, however, is that England's greatest defeat by Scotland in a football match has virtually been written out of our collective memory. For example, Lovesey (1993) wrote about great moments in British sport. A long list of outstanding sporting achievements were highlighted, such as the Tottenham Hotspur's double winning football team of 1961 and England's 1966 World Cup winning team. Even though Lovesey's work covered all the great sporting moments recorded from 1860-1992, no mention was made of England's heaviest defeat on home soil in 1881.

Two reasons help to explain why Watson's name seems to have been forgotten. Firstly, Watson played at a time when the game was essentially dominated by amateurs. Professional football was formally established in 1885 in England 1893 in Scotland. Notwithstanding this, he had a most distinguishable amateur career playing for the very best amateur clubs in Britain at that time, namely, Queen's Park of Glasgow and Corinthians based in London. In other words, he might not have been professional, but he played the game at the very highest level available which was comparable to any professional footballer playing at that time. Whilst Arthur Wharton can, therefore, be rightly considered as the first Black professional footballer in Britain, Watson very definitely preceded him by at least twelve years since he played for Parkgrove Football club in 1876 and had in fact been playing for Maxwell FC from about 1874. Many of the studies on the history football have tended to place much of their emphasis on the professional game and seem to ignore the very early period before professionalism.

In addition, most of Watson's football career took place in Scotland, and as the game developed and changed in terms of style and rules in England after the 1880s, Watson's worth, and those of other players north of the border, have received less attention as the game in England began to take pride of place within the British Isles. Yet, Scotland's 6-1 victory over England in 1881 was completely ignored, even though this was probably a more significant achievement, particularly since the game was played in London. Similarly, Galvin's work (2005) on football's greatest heroes focuses on those players and managers associated with the game in England. Therefore, the likes of Watson, who played for Scotland, even though he also played for English clubs, was not mentioned or highlighted in this compilation of great footballers.

The second reason for the paucity of information on Watson was that many of the books on the subject of the history of football in Britain, have tended to focus on the nature of the changes within the actual game, rather than the stand-out personalities who played. For example, Harvey (2005), Mason (1980) and Walvin, (1994b), are good cases in point which examine the general conditions or factors which influenced the development of football in Britain, without going into tremendous detail about individual personalities. Their focus have been on the changing nature of the socio-economic conditions, especially within the working class, or, the impact of the freeing-up of Saturday afternoons, as time off for workers, which corresponded with the growth in popularity of Saturday afternoon football games, or the impact of the football played in elite public schools. Many of the individuals involved in the playing of the game were not featured.

In fact, Taylor makes the point that 'academic writing on sport is sometimes assailed for neglecting what actually happens on the field of play' (Taylor, 2008, p. 85). If we accept the view of Fishwick, that social historians should not feel 'obliged to describe matches which they never saw or to engage in second-hand discussions of tactics...' (Taylor, 2008, p.85), we would never get to hear much about stand-out players and their influence on the game. This supports the point being made here, that because so many writers have focused on the wider context in which the game was being played and developed, though important in its own right, the players themselves become secondary and invisible.

In Walvin's work for example (1994b), his focus was on the development of the game by the end of the nineteenth century among the working classes. One of the many reasons cited for this was the increasing acceptance of the idea of Saturday afternoon holiday for workers especially in industrial cities in Britain after the 1860s (Walvin, 1994b, pp. 55, 56). According to Walvin, the most obvious consequence of this gradual introduction of the Saturday holiday for workers was that it allowed 'the industrial labour force to fill the free afternoons with organised recreation' (Walvin, 1994b, p. 56). For all these reasons, therefore, the contributions of Andrew Watson to the game of football in Scotland and England have largely been ignored.

One of the interesting points about the achievements of Watson, was the fact that as a Black person playing during the Victorian period in Britain, where discrimination against Black players was clearly evident, he seems to have experienced very little of such abuse and, if anything, endeared himself to the social elites in football and the wider British society. We are aware that he experienced some degree of 'vulgar abuse' from sections of the crowds in some matches, though it is not clear whether these were racist taunts. This, however, was not the same for a Black team mate of Watson in the 1870s named Robert Walker. As Chapter three shows, Walker played with Watson at Parkgrove Football Club in the mid 1870s, but certainly received some negative and discriminatory remarks concerning his ethnicity (McBrearty, 2015).

Garland and Rowe suggest that one of the problems associated with anti-racist campaigns in football is that the concept itself can sometimes be vague or unclear in its shades of meaning and interpretations. In fact, they point out that there are still debates pertaining to the very use of the term 'race' as a meaningful way to describe the indiscrimination experienced by Black people in football (Garland and Rowe, 2001, pp. 8-10). Despite this claim, however, the issues of racial discrimination towards Black sportsmen and women have been a feature of modern British society.

Perhaps, it could be argued that because Watson was so good, his Blackness or ethnicity became a non-issue. After all, according to one source, it was felt by some that;

> Sport is one field where ability and achievement can overcome prejudice...if a player can demonstrate he has the ability...that he might just win your team a few extra points in the season... he's in...in that sense football is incredibly democratic (Bains and Bowler, 2001, p. 25).

Therefore, because of his brilliance, or perhaps due to his general acceptability among the football and the social elites of his day, he might have experienced less of this racist abuse. There were, however, a number of outstanding Black sports people to whom this particular view, that their brilliance would see them over any hurdle, never materialised.

Speaking with reference to the 1970s when three prominent Black players, Batson, Cunningham and Regis played for West Bromwich Albion (the three degrees), the authors referred to a statement by the manager of the club at the time, Ron Atkinson, who was said to have remarked, that he was not keen on some of Black players in general who were unable to smile and ignore racist taunts from the crowds or from other players (Bains and Bowler, 2001, pp. 61, 62). This at least, suggests that racial discrimination was very much an experience which was encountered by Black players and goes against the earlier quote which suggests that in the face of true football brilliance, the game is very democratic. These three players were very good, but still experienced discrimination based on their Blackness or ethnicity. Therefore, while the game might have been democratic, it was not as anti-discriminatory in its practices and customs and verbal abuses meted out to people from different ethnic and cultural communities. One hundred years before the three degrees played for West Bromwich Albion, the same sort of behaviour was very much in evident in British football and sport in general.

For example, Arthur Wharton experienced a good deal of racial discrimination. He was considered by some newspaper reporters to have been good enough to play for England, but was overlooked. Garland and Rowe (2001) suggests that this was due to the desire on the part of the English FA of the 1880s and 1890s to insist on 'an ideal type of player' from the southern clubs (Garland and Rowe, 2001, p. 30). They cite an example where, on his arrival to play for Stalybridge Rovers in a game in 1896, a local newspaper used a hunting metaphor in commenting that the club had acquired the services of a 'real nigger as goalkeeper in Wharton, who was the darkie who used to guard the North End citadel' (Garland and Rowe, 2001). Galvin also informs us that newspapers routinely referred to Arthur Wharton as 'darkie' and occasionally questioned his intelligence. Furthermore, Wharton's 'physical and mental attributes as a player were often discussed in racial terms reflecting the debates in Victorian 'scientific' circles as to whether 'the Negro' was the intellectual equal of the Northern European' (Galvin, 2005, p. 4). Thus, as Garland and Rowe suggest, the early Black professional achieved their success despite the odds which were stacked against them in the form of considerable prejudice (Garland and Rowe, 2001, p. 33).

The level of racial discriminatory language and racial abuse was prevalent in the late nineteenth and early twentieth centuries in Britain. Walter Tull, who played for Spurs in 1909, was racially abused at a game at Bristol City and the headline in one newspaper stated 'problem of the colour prejudice.' According to Ismond, in order not to unsettle the rest of the team, the management at Spurs later got rid of Tull, first by demoting him to the reserves and then by off-loading him (Ismond, 2003, p. 25).

Perhaps one of the reasons why there have been very few, if any reported cases of racial abuse experienced by Watson during the late nineteenth century when he played, was because of the 'normalisation and under-reporting' of racial abuse prevalent in British society until fairly recent times. This normalisation of racism in football could also be seen more recently in Britain in a few highlighted cases. Firstly, in 1938 the England national football team played Germany in a friendly game. Before the start of the game the English players all gave the Nazi salute (Heatley, 2004, p. 45). Rather than focus on the politics associated with racism and the German Nazi Regime, England's victory of 6-3 was regarded as a sporting success and the political issue was dismissed or ignored as a major story of significance. The British Ambassador in Berlin warned one journalist in 1938, to be cautious about contests between German and British teams, mainly because the Nazi's were looking for easy opponents and victories to boost their regimes (Beck, 1999, p. 2). England's Stanley Matthews was reported to have said, the way the Germans viewed the match was as though it was a 'test of the New Order' (Beck, 1999, p. 6). As far as the English FA was concerned, the excuse or explanation for the Nazi Straight-arm salute was that it 'ensured a friendly reception by the huge crowd' and also created the 'right atmosphere' for the game (Beck, 1999, p. 6). Whilst some England players saw no harm in the salute, others felt it was in bad light, especially, as it was forced on them only minutes before the game was due to start. Eddie Hapgood, the England captain and also Stanley Matthews, were both shocked by this order which they were forced to carry out (Beck, 1999, p. 7).

A second example occurred in 1995 when Eric Cantona, the Manchester United footballer, reacted to taunts from the crowd by launching feet first at a spectator before exchanging punches with him. According to Ismond, Cantona snapped under a level of provocation which the vast majority of professional Black footballers endure with depressing frequency. The point seemed to be that some degree of response should be made where such discriminatory and racist behaviour is seen. According to Ismond, if Black players don't complain about racism which they feel oversteps personal boundaries of acceptability, they are simply legitimising this dimension of White-centred sports culture (Ismond, 2003, p. 18). However, even though a few high profile Black players such as Ian Wright and Stan Collymore have spoken out about the level of racial abuse by players, supporters and coaches, there is still a culture of denial amongst the very senior officials and managers within the game (Ismond, 2003, p. 18).

In the name of football, therefore, issues of racial discrimination could go un-noticed. For example, when the

Dutch Black footballer player Ruud Guillit was subjected to verbal abuse from sections of English supporters during the 1988 European Football Championships, a British commentator was reported to have said on live TV that Guillit was getting some good-natured barracking whenever he got possession of the ball (Ismond, 2003, p. 19). What this suggests, is that it seemed acceptable for spectators at football matches to use racist language and taunts towards Black players on the football pitch. However, if this kind of verbal abuse was being aimed at people in their place of work more generally in today's British society, there would be more of an outcry.

In fact, one of the features of racial discrimination in Britain during the trans-Atlantic slavery period and colonial era was a desire for there to be some degree of acceptance of this normalisation of racial discrimination. Walvin (1973) made reference to the fact that there was a belief among some White people that Black people should be content with their lot in society and not offer any resistance but be cheerfully obedient. He suggested that organised religion was often used by some people as a vehicle or system to ensure that Black people would not concentrate on the here and now, but focus on the life to come. For example, a morning prayer, which Walvin says was produced specially for the Black population in England in the eighteenth century said, 'O merciful God, grant that I may perform my duty this day faithfully and cheerfully; and that I may never murmur, be uneasy, or impatient under any of the troubles of this life' (Walvin, 1973, p. 69). Whilst it is not very clear to what extent Watson experienced such abuse or discrimination, what seems evident, was that his Blackness did not prevent him from achieving remarkable milestones.

At the time when Andrew Watson played for Scottish and English teams in the 1870s and 1880s, many people in Victorian Britain had already developed 'scientific' theories or explanations of 'race' based on a general correlation between anatomical features and mental psychological traits' (West, 1996, p. 20). According to West, the Victorian discourses on race consisted broadly of two competing views. Proponents of the first view centred their argument on the issue of 'humanitarian or civilising mission' with an emphasis on assimilation and the common origin of 'psychic unity of human being'. Proponents of the second perspective had accepted a more radical account with its focus on the fact that 'the races had separate origins, and distinct, unequal characteristics' (West, 1996, p. 23). Either way, many Black people were considered unequal to White people and thus subject to discriminatory taunts and practices especially within Britain during the last quarter of the nineteenth century.

There are two key points which should be noted at this juncture. Firstly, despite these discriminatory attitudes and practices in the late nineteenth century, Black people had a long tradition of participating in sports. Secondly, racial discrimination against Black people was not exclusive to the sport of football, but existed in a number of other sports. There can be little doubt that from very early in the history of human development, ancient civilisations were involved in a wide range of sporting activities. As humans 'trained animals and manufactured means of transport, so horses, camels, llamas, elephants were raced and oarsmen tested their strength and timing against each other' (Hutchinson, 1996, p. 19). From Mesopotamia through Greece, Africa and Asia, there was evidence of organised sport. From drawings in Mesopotamia, there was evidence of swimming, wrestling and horse-racing. The Olympic Games are, of course, closely associated with Ancient Greece. Athletics, wrestling, gymnastics, chariot-racing were among some of the popular sports which took place during these ancient games.

In terms of the involvement of Black people in sports more specifically, this was evident in ancient Egypt, where, from as early as 1160 BC, there was indication of art work showing well-dressed spectators watching pairs of 'multiracial' wrestlers, and groups of stick-fighters. There were also images of boys playing tug-of-war, as well as jumping over high bars, lifting heavy sandbags, under water swimming, and rowing (Hutchinson, 1996, p. 20). The Egyptian nobles and soldiers were very actively engaged in such sports as running, hunting and strenuous performances involving men and women making use of ball games and also board games (Kyle, 2015, p. 26). What is evident from these depictions of sport in ancient Egypt was that they valued leisure time and, according to Hutchinson, even their children's tombs contained balls of packed straw bound in coloured leather or balls of wood and of baked clay (Hutchinson, 1996, p. 20). Because so many of the forms of evidence of Egyptian games have been derived from drawings on the tombs of the rich, Kyle has warned that many of the sports are therefore showing the sporting activities of the elite (Kyle, 2015, p. 27). Part of the reason for such an emphasis in Egypt was because their Pharaohs were supposed to demonstrate not only spiritual well-being, but also physical perfection. For this reason, there were many images of pharaohs actively engaged in sports such as the Sed Festivals in which they were expected to run on foot, around a long particular circuit which was partly a symbolic ritual to demonstrate that the pharaoh was physically fit to rule (Kyle, 2015, p. 27).

There is some suggestion that sporting activity within ancient societies might have been linked to the need for human survival. For example, hunting of animals was probably needed long before the skills needed for hunting became associated with sports. In effect, therefore, many eventual sporting events were, the continuation of rituals associated with specific skills. Various Mesopotamian texts from Ur suggest physical performances associated with festivals at royal courts (Kyle, 2015, pp. 24, 25).

The second point which has to be briefly noted was that it was not only in the game of football that Black people excelled in the late nineteenth century and early twentieth centuries without getting the recognition they deserved. The examples of two outstanding Black sports people serve to demonstrate this. The first of these individuals was Peter Jackson who was known as the 'Black Prince' and, was born in St Croix, part of the Danish West Indies in 1861. He later moved to Australia with his fisherman father, where, in 1886, he became the heavy weight boxing champion of Australia and the world. Jackson's family had originated from Montego Bay in Western Jamaica, and he himself died in 1901. Similar to Andrew Watson, Jackson's story started in the Caribbean and ended in a different part of the world, where he made a name for himself. It is just a pity that this Caribbean-born boxer, was not able to realise his full potential within his sport, partly resulting from the racist and discriminatory practices which were common place in Britain and elsewhere in the industrialised world in the late nineteenth century.

It is such a travesty of history that the place where sports super stars are born and grew up becomes overshadowed by the achievements in their subsequent adopted homes. It is even worse that they are often not recognised at all. Clyde Best, born in Bermuda and Jamaican-born John Barnes are two cases who would fit this kind of categorisation where their places of birth are often ignored in discussions about their sporting success. In the field of boxing, the remarkable achievements of Peter Jackson also serve as an excellent example of this pattern. According to Peterson, Peter's father, Joseph Jackson, was a carpenter born into slavery and his wife's name was Julia. Peter had ninety nine fights with only three losses and four draws (Peterson, 2011).

As Garland and Rowe assert, many Black sports people were seen as 'exotic' show-pieces for entertainment and thus not often taken very seriously by large sections of the White population (Garland and Rowe, 2001, p. 31). This was certainly true of Peter Jackson, where, he was first denied opportunities to fight the very best boxing champions on the grounds that Black and White boxers could not fight in the same ring. In his later years, he travelled from Australia to the USA in attempts to find suitable opponents to compete with, before ending his days as an entertainer on the stage.

According to Susan Clark (2000), Jackson's disillusionment in the boxing ring, on the stage and in American society, was related to the racist ideology that predominated in these societies. Jackson's boxing career, which started in 1882 when he was 21 years of age, really came to prominence when he defeated Jack Hayes in a seven round bout. By 1886 Jackson defeated Tom Lees, the then Australian Heavy weight champion of Australia. However, when the Australian Jack Burke refused to fight Jackson on the grounds that he did not want to ruin his reputation by fighting a Black man, Jackson decided to travel to the United States to further his boxing career by trying to find suitable opponents (Clark, 2000). One of the key points from this article by Clark is that the sport of boxing served as a symbol among some White people of not only their superiority in general, but also of their superiority in sports. As Clark points out, the White population had more to lose from having the prospect of a Black man beating a White man in a boxing ring. When, eventually Jackson was able to fight against a White opponent in the person of Joe McAuliffe in December 1888, following his arrival in the USA, and defeated him, the Black community in San Francisco was euphoric.

As it became increasingly difficult for Jackson to find suitable opponents, his management tried to make him more appealing to the wider community and tried to portray him as a soft-spoken, mildly mannered gentleman (Clark, 2000, p. 161). Eventually, Jackson ended his boxing career and toured all over America as part of the play 'Uncle Tom'. Jackson was denied the opportunity to become the world heavyweight champion but instead became a humiliating spectacle in a play where Black people were stereotyped for their brainless athleticism or entertainers.

Of course this was not the first time that a Black boxer found himself up against the wrath and racist discrimination from White opponents. Tom Molineaux was born in Virginia, USA in 1784, and started his boxing career by fighting on the plantations primarily as an entertainer for the plantation owners. He eventually bought his freedom and, after boxing in New York, came to London, where, in 1810, he fought for the British heavyweight championship title against Tom Cribb but was controversially and unfairly beaten. The re-match in 1811 was also controversially decided in Cribb's favour. Molineaux died in 1818 in relatively poverty in Dublin, Ireland.

What was interesting about this fight between Cribb and Molineaux was the significance of racial discrimination he had to endure. According to David Leafe, writing in the Mail online (2010), Molineaux had only two fights to his name on British soil and, had made history just by being in the same ring. He was, in fact, the first Black person to fight for the British heavyweight championship. Furthermore, Molineaux's trainer, Bill Richmond, known as the 'Black terror' was also a former slave born in New York in 1763, as well as a boxer. Richmond had developed a good reputation as a boxer and was earning one hundred guineas a fight (Leafe, 2010). Richmond had himself fought against Cribb in 1805 but was beaten by him. Richmond, however, remained in the sport by becoming a boxing trainer and it was in this way that he became the Molineaux's trainer. In the end, though, both men failed to realise their fortunes in the sport of boxing.

From the discussions above, it becomes clear that the argument that an outstanding sports star will somehow generally be able to overcome any obstacle and achieve great success, regardless of any abuse they might experience, was not always the case for many Black sports people. Arthur Wharton, who played from the late 1880s and 1890s, had great ability as a goal-keeper and was certainly good enough to have played for England. He was, at one time, playing for Preston North End, which was one of the very best football teams in England. The three degrees who played for West Bromwich during the 1970s also demonstrates this point. They faced a great deal of racist abuse when they played. It has only been in the last twenty or thirty years that very serious measures have been taken in Britain to eliminate such racist language and behaviour from the game. Organisations like 'KickitOut' based in the UK, have specifically been established to address these kinds of issues.

Although there is still room for improvement, more Black people are doing extremely well within sports in Britain today because of the various legislations and a general improvement in acceptable levels of behaviour in the last two decades. During the time Watson played in the 1870s and 1880s, however, this was not the case. Furthermore, a good deal of the racist behaviour was normalised to such an extent, that many Black players were prevented from reaching their full sporting potential. In other words, largely as a result of the prevailing discriminatory practices in Britain, sports stars like Richmond and Molineaux were denied their opportunities to excel even more than they did. It was truly a rare thing, therefore, for a

Black person to have accomplished so much sporting success during the late nineteenth century in Britain. That Watson was able to achieve so much within this political climate during Victorian times, when so many other notable and exceptional Black sports people were unable to, demonstrates why he deserves special credit.

Conclusion

Andrew Watson, though not apparently personally victimised by significant racial discrimination, was able to rise to the very highest possible status within his sport. This, however, was the not the case for a number of other notable Black footballers during the Victorian period and even much later in twentieth century in Britain. From the foregoing, it is clear that despite the odds which were heavily stacked against them, many Black sports people could still achieve outstanding levels of standards and accomplishments and thereby compete with the very best in the world. However, despite their personal skills and abilities, many of these Black sports people were not appreciated or truly recognised or acknowledged for their remarkable accomplishments. As a result of the various forms of discrimination levelled against some of these players, they were robbed of their opportunity to excel to the very highest levels within their sport. This is what makes the Watson story even more remarkable. Andrew Watson's achievement deserves to be recognised and celebrated and this becomes even more apparent in the next chapter which provides a fuller biography of his life and football career.

CHAPTER THREE

Background and Biography of a Caribbean-Born Football Superstar

The primary purpose of this chapter is to examine the extraordinary achievements of Andrew Watson, especially with regard to his football career. The chapter also provides some background into the two different countries which had a great impact on Watson's life, Guyana in the Caribbean, and Glasgow in Scotland. This is important as it helps to provide the crucial underpinning and historical context for much of the subsequent analysis. Watson's claim to fame, in terms of his footballing technical ability and business involvement in the game, can be based on the number of firsts which he personally achieved. The fact that Watson was a player in great demand by all the top teams of his day, would certainly have earned him the distinction of being described as the world's first Black football superstar. Despite his rather illustrious career, however, Watson's story had more humble beginnings, thousands of miles away on the South American mainland British Caribbean colony of Guyana.

Guyana at the Time of Watson's Birth

Although the Republic of Guyana is on the South American mainland, its history is closely linked with that of the rest of the Caribbean. The history and development of the Caribbean over the last five hundred years, has been shaped and influenced greatly by European colonialism, plantation slavery and resistance struggles, be they political, economic or socio-cultural, to exercise varying degrees of self-determination. Before the arrival of Columbus and the Spanish to the Caribbean region at the end of the fifteenth century, the entire

Americas was dominated by a variety of local Indians or 'Amerindians.' For most of the Caribbean region, these peoples, variously called Tainons, Caribs, Siboney, etc, lived in relatively independent communities, with their economies based primarily on fishing and agricultural cultivation of crops such as cassava as well as sweet potatoes and maize.

Following its political independence in 1966, the name Guyana was adopted as the official designation of this independent nation. Accordingly, the name Guyana has been used throughout this book, rather than its previous name, British Guiana. Guyana was the name of the colony on the north eastern coast of the South American mainland which shared a similar or common history with the rest of Britain's Caribbean island territories. Although this country is located on the northeast of the South American continent, it is the only English speaking member of the Caribbean to be located there. At the time Guyana gained its political independence from Britain in 1966, its main economic features were fairly similar to most of the other Caribbean societies. There was a very heavy dependence on a few agricultural commodities and, or mineral exports. In the case of Guyana the principal export earners were bauxite-alumina, rice and sugar. In fact, during the period 1960-1985 bauxite-alumina accounted for about 20% of the country's economy at its peak (Thomas, 1988, p. 105). By the 1970s, the country declared itself a Cooperative Socialist Republic. Although no longer a socialist country today, Guyana has had a much older, albeit short-lived experience, attempting to adopt a socialist path of development. According to C.Y. Thomas (1988) when the first Guyanese elections, based on universal adult suffrage resulted in the first freely elected Marxist government in the British Empire in 1953, the country's constitution was suspended by the British Government after only one hundred and thirty three days (Thomas, 1988, pp. 60-61).

Despite Spain's attempt to establish a trade monopoly where they could dominate the production of goods produced in the Caribbean region and market these to the rest of Europe, they were never able to police and take effective control of such a vast geographical entity. This allowed the Dutch, English and French settlers and colonialists to subsequently take control of the islands primarily in the Eastern Caribbean by the beginning of the seventeenth century. This general trend, of other European countries taking away more and more of these Caribbean territories from Spain, as well as the loss of other Spanish territory through the revolutionary independence movements in the early nineteenth century, especially in South America, resulted in the global decline and marginalisation of Spain as a major international colonial power. The other European states which had settled in the Caribbean in the seventeenth century had, by the middle of that century, after having experimented with different export commodities, such as tobacco, succeeded in producing sugar, which became the principal export crop from the Caribbean. The introduction of this single crop would fundamentally change the global economic and political significance of the Caribbean. Guyana, in this respect, shares the same general history as the rest of the British Caribbean, in that it became part of the wealth–making Caribbean bases for the British imperial power.

The first Europeans to colonise the country were the Dutch, who establish three separate colonies of Berbice, Demerara and Essequibo. The indigenous peoples of the country consisted of Indians or Amerindians, some of whom were believed to have moved north out of South America into the Eastern Caribbean. Thus, by the time Columbus and the Spanish arrived in the Caribbean towards the end of the fifteenth century, these were the people they encountered. The country was finally ceded to the British from the Dutch in 1814 through the Treaty of Paris. In 1831 the three colonies were joined together as one sovereign state then called British Guiana. Following the ending of slavery in 1834 and the apprenticeship system four years later, Guyana's economy was so dependent upon African slave labour, that there was a chronic labour shortage as the ex-slaves generally sought to move away from relations with their former masters which tied them to working on lands for them. It therefore became necessary to engage the services of indentured East Indian workers. This large-scale arrival of tens of thousands of

Indian labourers from the 1830s until the first few years of the twentieth century ultimately changed the demographic make-up of the country. Today, just over half the population of Guyana are of East Indian origin. Therefore, the arrival of East Indians had a profound effect on the country. With the planters unable to secure readily reliable supply of labourers, it was feared that the colony would tread the 'path of an inescapable doom' (Ruhomon, 1988, p. 8). The main reason for this grim mood was the lack of an adequate labour force for the key agricultural production upon which the country, like most other Caribbean territories at that time, were so dependent. In 1838 the first two ships from Calcutta arrived in Guyana with four hundred and six Indians on board who were to be the first of the countless waves of Indian indentured labourers to arrive in Guyana (Ruhomon, 1988, p. 26).

Although Guyana might not always receive a great deal of attention as the rest of the Caribbean islands, its history was extremely important both within the wider Caribbean context as well as to the British economy in the nineteenth century. David Alston's work shows that up to one-eighth of all slaves in the British Caribbean at the time of emancipation in 1834 were in Guyana. Furthermore, because of the high demand for labour there, relative to the other Caribbean territories, a quarter of all compensation paid to British plantation owners went to those owning slaves in Guyana (Alston, 2014, pp.1, 2). More specifically, with regard to our interests with Scotland, there were significant numbers of Scottish residents in Guyana, or absentee Scottish owners living in Britain, who were owners of businesses in Guyana. Alston believes that of the two thousand five hundred White colonists in Demerara and Essequibo in 1810, at least one thousand were likely to have been Scottish (Alston, 2014a, p. 8). Furthermore, by 1819 one in fifty of the enslaved population of Berbice was the child or grandchild of a White European (Alston, 2014, p. 14).

The extent of Scottish presence and influence in Guyana in the nineteenth century can be seen with regard to the significance of the presence of the Church of Scotland. There was such a substantial Scottish community in Guyana, that the Church of

Scotland was also officially supported financially by the Colonial Government in England. This meant there were two state churches in Guyana, one being the Church of England, while the other was the Church of Scotland (Moore, 1995, p. 39). For most of the period after emancipation in the nineteenth century, the colonial elites of Guyana were mainly Scottish, English and Irish immigrants serving a wide variety of occupations from book-keepers and overseers on the estates, to merchants, lawyers, doctors, priests, police and colonial officials, and there was also a substantial group of local-born whites who formed 42-45% of the total white population (Moore, 1998, pp. 96, 97). This is a point which we come back to below in this chapter, when we look at Andrew Watson's family in Guyana, who could trace their roots in the country to the very early nineteenth century.

In terms of the manner in which the social and recreational activities of the wealthy White elites in the Caribbean were observed, these followed similar patterns as those commonly practised in Britain during the Victorian period. As was the case in Britain, the rich and powerful Whites spent a good deal of their leisure time in such activities as indoor games, like chess and cards, as well as reading rooms, entrance to which, were reserved for the exclusive White membership. Although they were in the Caribbean, the White elites did everything to maintain aspects of the British Victorian culture (Moore, 1998, p. 101). However, in Guyana in the middle of the nineteenth century there were very few institutions or places to stimulate intellectual and artistic life, suitable for such White British-based elites. There was a small public library, a grammar school called Queen's College, and the Berbice Reading Society (Moore, 1998, p. 104). In Guyana intellectual activity was often secondary to the pursuit of economic wealth, but by 1844 the Queens College was founded. Its curriculum, not surprisingly followed the main curriculum path of the public schools in England and its teachers were mainly products of the English public school system. Moore informs us that for the entire duration of the nineteenth century, the student population was very small and very elite and its total student numbers never exceeded seventy (Moore, 1995, p. 58).

More generally, there were very few places of entertainment such as theatres or cinemas suitable for the White elites. It should come as no surprise, therefore, that those who could afford it, sent their children to Britain to be educated. This is exactly what happened in the case of Andrew Watson, as his father eventually sent him for education and up-bringing in Britain. Furthermore, sexual promiscuity, or the indulgences or even excesses of the 'white stud' or 'lady-killer' were rampant among the colonial elites beyond the end of the nineteenth century, and for a young man to lead a regular and virtuous life, would expose them ridicule by society (Moore, 1998, p. 103). For Peter Miller Watson, the father of Andrew Watson, to have had a child with a local Black woman in Guyana would not, therefore, have raise significant news or surprise.

An important feature of Watson's life was his social background and the role of elitism in sports. Wealth, affluence and social prestige were not only present in Victorian Britain, but also in Guyana and the rest of the Anglophone Caribbean. According to Moore (1998), social snobbery and luxurious life styles were rife and had been brought to Guyana and the rest of the Caribbean by the colonists from Britain. The new found wealth obtained in the Caribbean meant many White people could find a short cut to social elevation, and because of the small size of the White planter elites in the colonies, this meant everyone knew everyone else, therefore making it important not to be seen in the wrong crowd or association (Moore, 1998, p. 98). Moore points out that the White elites in Guyana tried to dress in the same style, using the same material as those which were popular in England and which of course, were not really suited for the tropics.

The White elites made every effort to copy aspects of Victorian culture and replicate these in the Caribbean. In terms of social culture as well, by the late nineteenth century, the Scottish community in Guyana celebrated St Andrews Day on 30 November with a splendid show of fashions and part of the day's celebrations, consisted of a church service followed by large dinner parties and dancing parties or balls, where mainly Scottish music was played (Moore, 1995, p. 29). Moore also makes the point that the White elites of Guyana spent a great deal of their time in leisure activities especially taking walks along the promenade near the sea front. For example the Georegtown Club, founded in 1858 which was part of the Assembly Room, was one place where the wealthy could meet and socialise. The Assembly Rooms were built in 1858 as the main venue for the high society balls, concerts and dinners.

It was perfectly natural that because of the development of sports in Britain in the late nineteenth century, these ideas would, in time, spread to the Caribbean colonies. This was certainly the case in Andrew Watson's country of birth. For the White colonialists, one advantage of taking part in sports was that it helped many of them to 'express and enhance the solidarity of colonial society' as well as for providing 'amusement for those from home, isolated within a hostile population' (Moore, 1998, p. 107). What this meant, was that it became the norm for certain elite sports like cricket, rugby and football, to be played among the White elites in the Caribbean. Because of Guyana's large forest and wildlife resources, it helped to provide the British aristocrats with ample opportunities to engage in the elite sport of hunting which was both prestigious and also a very expensive pastime. A hunting trip of three or four days could cost a party of four people as much as $25.00 per head (Moore, 1998, p. 109).

Another important issue which is a central theme in this book centres on the debate between those who supported professionalism and those who preferred amateurism with regard to sports. There was a very definite distinction between amateur and professional sports in Guyana as well as the wider Caribbean. The middle class gentlemen considered it degrading to engage in the playing of sports for any kind of payment. This was an idea in the Caribbean which had emanated from the White colonial elites who came to settle in these countries in the eighteenth and nineteenth centuries. As we will see in chapter six of this study, it was the elites within British society who argued the longest and hardest for the promotion and continuation of the spirit of amateurism. The rich and powerful were seen as people who engaged in sport and leisure activities as marks of social standing and distinction, rather than as means to generate income. As Moore pointed out, payment was for the lower orders, with no other source of income. More broadly, similar ideas about class and sports was seen in the colonies as, many Whites simply refused to take part in any sporting event where Black people were involved (Moore, 1995, p. 68). In this sense, therefore, sports was used a form of cultural assimilation in that some aspects of British cultural values and standards and conformity were transferred through such activities. The most popular sport introduced by the British to Guyana was, of course, cricket. The Georgetown Cricket Club was founded in 1852 and is the oldest elite cricket club in the Caribbean. This club was founded for, and composed mainly of, the plantocracy and government officials. This was a game based on strict discipline and the obedience of law and order issued by the team captain was, in itself, very symbolic of the Victorian values which were so ingrained in British society at this time.

The economic mainstay of the country in the nineteenth century was the agricultural production of sugar, coffee and cotton, and this was made possible by the abundant supply of African slaves to which the census of 1817 suggested numbered one hundred and ten thousand. In 1829 there was reported to be two hundred and thirty sugar and one hundred and seventy four coffee and cotton estates (Ruhomon, 1988, p. 9). Until the 1880s the plantation sector accounted for over 90% of the total export trade (Moore, 1998, p. 97). However, as a result of the Emancipation Act, and the loss of labourers on the estates, many plantations and even roads were found to be in a state of neglect (Ruhomon, 1988, pp. 11-14).

However, there were signs of economic activity among the ex-slaves in Guyana. From the period after slavery and the Apprenticeship, Black people in Guyana were able to pool their financial resources and purchase property and were able to establish villages including Buxton, Friendship and Victoria. Some one hundred and forty one people bought Plantation Orange Nassau and renamed it Buxton and they did this by contributing sums ranging from $1000, $362, $350 and $36. (Josiah, 2011, p. 13).

At the time of Andrew Watson's birth in Guyana in the 1850s, therefore, the country was trying to recover from the economic shocks and difficulties which were being experienced as a result of these declining agricultural productive sectors. A Select Committee of 1842 had already concluded that the exodus of African labourers from the estates in their numbers was the principle cause behind the diminished production and the economic distress, which was being experienced throughout the larger British Caribbean colonies of Guyana, Jamaica and the Trinidad and Tobago (Ruhomon, 1988, p. 16). In Guyana, it was the arrival of East Indians in large numbers after 1838 that enabled the sugar plantation industry to survive. By the late 1850s and early 1860s as Andrew Watson was being prepared to be sent to Britain, the population of the country was undergoing dramatic social and demographic changes due to the arrival of the East Indians. It was, therefore, from such a Caribbean and more specifically, Guyanese background, that Andrew Watson was born.

Biography of Watson

Andrew Watson was born in Georgetown Guyana in 1856 to a Scottish plantation owner named Peter Miller Watson and a local Guyanese Black woman named Hannah Rose. Peter Watson was born on 6 June 1805 in Kiltearn in Scotland and died in Surrey on 22 April 1869. It seems reasonably evident, albeit from fragments of scanty indications available, that he was a considerably wealthy individual, and was the owner of a property and at least sixteen slaves in Guyana during the mid to late 1830s. This can be established from the compensation payments he received following the legal ending of slavery in the British Caribbean in 1834 which had been agreed as part of the Emancipation Act. As part of the conditions for the British Parliament reluctantly agreeing to this Act, British-based Caribbean plantation owners were to collectively receive twenty Million Pounds Sterling as compensation for the loss of earnings which, in effect, was payments for every slave they owned at the time. Peter Watson was one of the Caribbean plantation owners who received payment for sixteen slaves.

It is largely due to the initial research and subsequent website, produced by the University College London (UCL) on the compensation paid to such plantation owners, that it has been possible to ascertain the details about Peter Watson's actual compensation pay outs (UCL, 2016, Legacies of British Slave Ownership). From this record, it appears that Peter Watson made four separate claims for compensation of the slaves he owned in Guyana. It appears that two separate claims were recorded on 14 December 1835. One of these claims was for two slaves for which he received £126. He also received another pay out of £223 for another six slaves. On the 1 February 1836, he received £166 for three slaves and finally, on 6 February 1836 he received £299 for five slaves (UCL, 2016, Legacies of British Slave Ownership). Therefore, according to these records, he received just over £800 for his sixteen slaves.

From David Alston's website on the connections between Highland Scots and Guyana, we learn that Peter Watson also had three brothers who were also from Scotland. Two of them are significant for our purposes, precisely because they eventually went to live and work in Guyana. Henry (Harry) Watson was born in 1801 and died in 1836 while his younger brother Andrew Watson, was born in 1803 and died in 1837. Both of these men were also compensated for the loss of their slaves following the Emancipation Act in 1834. Harry was compensated for his seven slaves, while Andrew was compensated for six slaves (Alston, *Slaves and Highlanders*). Both these men also eventually died in Guyana. Peter Watson, however, returned to Britain in 1858, two years after he had fathered an illegitimate child called Andrew Watson. Not only were Andrew Watson's father and two uncles strongly connected to Guyana, but their father, that is, Andrew Watson's grandfather, James Watson, had married Christian Robertson. It turns out, that this family had also already established strong links with Guyana. James Watson himself died in 1808. Thus, if we incorporate the Robertson family, we can see that at least three generations of Andrew Watson's family lived in Guyana. It is quite likely that since

Andrew Watson's father had a brother called Andrew, this might be the source or influence behind the choosing of his son's name of Andrew.

Although Andrew Watson was regarded as an illegitimate child, his father at least sought to ensure his personal well-being. What is not clear from any of the records examined from the Guyana National archives is the history or fate of Andrew Watson's mother who was called Hannah or Anna Rose. What seems clear, however, is that Watson and his older Sister Annetta, were sent to England. The fact that Andrew Watson's father sent him to very prestigious education institutions helped to provide Watson with a very privileged educational background. This, as is discussed later in this book, was a critical factor in his subsequent involvement with the development football as a player for the socially elite team, called Corinthians of London. His privileged background is demonstrated from the fact that he attended three of the finest education institutions at that time in the form of Heath School in West Yorkshire, King's College in London and then Glasgow University. This, along with the fact that his father left £35,000 for him in his will, meant Watson was able to enjoy some of the privileges normally associated and reserved for the very social elites in British society.

According to the sports historian Andy Mitchell, the money left for Andrew Watson after Peter Watson's death in 1869, of £35,000, meant Watson (and his sister) had financial security (Mitchell, 2013). At today's rate this would be equivalent to over £3 million pounds. Soon after his arrival in England, Andrew Watson, now aged ten years of age, was admitted to the Heath Grammar School in August 1866 by the school's head, Dr Thomas Cox. It was also possible that he might have lived at the Crossley Orphan Home which was also associated with the school (Taylor, Kafel and Smith, 2006, p. 36). His attendance at a home of this nature would certainly not have been uncommon, given the fact that Andrew Watson was an illegitimate child, and might not have had tremendous personal contact with his father. These two educational establishments would later merge to form the Crossley Heath School in

Halifax, West Yorkshire, and which was a very prestigious institution which first opened in the year 1600.

Andrew Watson was also a pupil at the King's College School in London, which had been established in 1829 as a junior department of the then newly established King's College, part of the University of London. Although his father was financially supporting Watson's education in Britain, it appears, from discussions with senior staff at the school associated with the school's archives, regarding the original records of Andrew Watson's admission, that Peter Watson's name does not appear on any of the paper work associated with his son's school admission. This means Andrew Watson was registered by somebody else, we assume on the father's behalf. This again, is probably further evidence of his father providing financial support for Andrew Watson, but delegating such matters to someone else who he would no doubt have arranged for such a purpose. It appears, therefore, that his father was certainly providing legal and financial support, though perhaps, not as much emotional support. What is clear, however, is that Andrew Watson was a pupil at this school. This was, and still is, a very prestigious secondary school. During the 1860s and 1870s many students from this institution would go to engage in further studies at either Oxford or Cambridge Universities. Even today, King's College is still regarded as one of the very top independent schools in the country, with a significant number of students still going on to further their education at Oxbridge Universities. Although Watson started his degree programme at the University of Glasgow, he did not complete his studies, but went on to concentrate increasingly on playing football. It was only after his football playing career that he eventually returned to the completion of his formal training and qualification in engineering.

That Watson should have received such privileged treatment was not unusual during this period of British colonial history. Because of the tremendous wealth generated by Caribbean plantation owners who were originally from Scotland and England, many of them rose in social standing and were able to send their children (especially the boys) to some of the best schools in England and Scotland. Furthermore, it was also becoming increasingly common for Scottish Plantation owners to send their children back to Scotland to receive formal education. Many of these children were fathered by white Scots men who had Black mistresses, thus giving rise to the number of 'mulatto' children who later found themselves in Scotland. John Robertson of Tobago for example, paid for the board and lodgings for Charles and Daniel Robertson, two mulatto boys, so they could live in Britain (Hamilton, 2005, p. 210).

Many mulatto, mixed-race or dual heritage children born of Scottish fathers and Guyanese enslaved women received their education in Scotland. Children from Guyana attended schools in the Highlands of Inverness, Fortrose, Tain and Dornoch, Dollar, Paisley, as well as Glasgow, Liverpool and London (Alston, 2014a, p. 22). Nor were all these children readily accepted by their Scottish White peers in the schools within Scotland. This can be seen from the way Hugh Miller reflected on his school days with mulatto children in the Scottish Highland of Dornoch around 1815. 'There was' he said, 'a mulatto lad who sat in his form who was not only older and stouter than the other children in class, but also 'dreaded by the other boys for a wild savage disposition which is, I believe, natural to his country-folk (Alston, 2014a p. 21).

In addition, one hundred and forty eight students from the Caribbean were enrolled at Eton College between 1753 and 1776, compared with only twenty two from the thirteen North American colonies (Hamilton, 2005, p. 209). Between 1731 and 1810, one hundred and nineteen students from the Caribbean matriculated at Glasgow University while at Edinburgh University, one hundred and fourteen students from the Caribbean graduated in medicine between 1744 and 1810 (Hamilton, 2005, pp. 210, 211). One such son of the Caribbean who went to study in Scotland was of course, Andrew Watson. In 1875 he moved from London to study mathematics, natural philosophy, civil engineering at Glasgow University, but after a year he left there to go a work as an engineering apprentice. He married Jessie Armour in 1877 and they had two children. The 1881 census showed that Andrew Watson and his wife and child lived at Afton Crescent in Govan, Scotland.

Illustration 1: St. Ninian's Church on Albert Drive, Glasgow, where Andrew Watson first got married. (Photo by T. Talburt August 2015)

Illustration 2: Another image of the St Ninian's Church where Watson first got married. (Photo by T. Talburt, August 2015)

That Watson's father should be a Scottish man with Caribbean plantation business was also not abnormal during the eighteenth and nineteenth centuries. By the middle of the eighteenth century, Scottish towns like Glasgow had flourishing manufacturing industries which were linked to the North American and Caribbean colonial or slave trades. In the Glasgow tobacco trades, as well as the Caribbean sugar and cotton trades, there was a corresponding increase in demand for storage and merchandising facilities in the docks of Glasgow. In fact, between 1765 and 1795 Hamilton claimed there was a ten-fold increase of Scottish linen exports to Jamaica, arising mainly from the need to meet the demand for coarse osnaburg cloth for slave garments (Hamilton, 2005, p. 15). Furthermore, it appears that there were a considerable number of Scottish plantation owners or overseers, and a Scottish community along the Demerara River even before the country was ceded to Britain following the Napoleonic wars in 1815.

Glasgow is significant for this study not only because this was a very important trading and manufacturing town linked to colonial overseas trade, but also because this was where Andrew Watson lived and played his football in Scotland. It was also from Glasgow, that Queen's Park Football Club was established which played a very significant role in the development of the modern game in Scotland. In terms of its economic significance, Tom Devine informs us that in the middle decades of the eighteenth century, tobacco formed just less than half of all Scottish imports from outside the United Kingdom in terms of value, and most of this was channelled through the Port of Clydesdale in Glasgow (Devine, 1990). So important was this single trade industry in Glasgow, that in the very preface to this book, Devine made the statement that Glasgow was Scotland as far as the tobacco trade was concerned. More broadly, however, the evidence of overseas colonial trade in Glasgow was clearly visible on many of the main roads in the city. There were scores of warehouses, merchant buildings, shops and refineries. All the main commodities connected with the colonial trade, ranging from the transatlantic slave trade, sugar, cotton, tea, tobacco could be found in Glasgow.

The tobacco trade was certainly one important area in which the merchants in Glasgow were so dominant in numbers that in

1778, in a plan of the city, only churches and manufacturing buildings or establishments rivalled the town mansions of the tobacco aristocracy, in terms of size and architectural appeal. Furthermore, these tobacco merchants dominated the political life of the city, until almost the end of the eighteenth century with most of the merchant councillors actually being tobacco merchants. Not only were these merchants focusing on tobacco from North America, but most of these Glasgow traders were also closely associated with the commercial businesses in such provisions as fish, wheat, rice, and cotton. What this meant, was that many of these merchants were also buying and selling goods all over North America as well as the Caribbean (Devine, 1990, pp. 11-13). That Scotland in general, and Glasgow in particular, were connected by trade and commerce to overseas colonial trade, could also be seen from an examination of some of the major roads or streets in the city. Jamaica Street and St Vincent Street were two examples of places which gave some indication of the source from which a great deal of wealth was coming into the city. For example, Robert Baird was a business man in Glasgow who was a brass founder in 1877 and his business address was at Kinning Park, at a number 20 Plantation Place. These street names give some indication of the significance of the Caribbean to Glasgow during the eighteenth and nineteenth centuries.

The eighteenth and nineteenth centuries witnessed the rapid growth in the size and number of industrial towns and cities both north and south of the Scottish border. One of the effects of the Industrial Revolution in Britain was that it led to the dramatic increase in the urban population. In 1700 there were believed to be an estimated five and a half million people living in England and Wales, and this increased to nearly nine million by 1801, when the first official census was done. By the middle of the nineteenth century this had doubled to nearly eighteen million people (Rose, 1985, p. 276). There was a similar pattern in Scotland. The population grew from 1.7 million in 1755 to nearly 3 million by 1851. The growth of towns such as Liverpool, Manchester and Glasgow as well as other industrial towns in northern England and southern Scotland, was a major attraction for immigrant and migrant workers and settlers a like (Rose, 1985, p. 277).

For Andrew Watson in particular, and for Black people more generally, living in towns like Glasgow in the second half of the nineteenth century would not have been a totally unusual occurrence. Significant numbers of Black people had been present in Scotland from at least the beginning of the sixteenth century. According to James Walvin, for example, there were a number of Africans at the court of King James 1V of Scotland about 1500 A.D. (Walvin, 1994a, p. 83). Peter Fryer, referring to the same example, highlighted the fact that there was an African drummer and choreographer to whom the King seemed very fond (Fryer, 1984, p. 2). The Black eighteenth century anti-slavery campaigner and author, Olaudah Equiano had, among his subscribers for the sixth edition of his book in 1793, four hundred and eighty seven subscribers in England, sixty eight in Ireland and one hundred and fifty eight in Scotland (Fryer, 1984, p. 110). This indicates the extent to which the issue of slavery, and the campaigns against it, exorcised the minds of significant numbers in Scotland who were certainly aware of the exploitation of many Black people in their presence. What the preceding paragraphs help to demonstrate is that industrialised cities or towns like Glasgow were linked with the overseas trades in the Caribbean and North America, and, would have been places where small, but significant numbers of Black people would have also lived. The majority of these Black people, as was the case in England, were often employed as servants in the house-holds of the very rich or were students in the main schools and universities. Andrew Watson's situation was, however, very significantly different. And the reason for his unique situation arose from his involvement in the sport of football in Glasgow.

Watson's football career in Scotland started when he played for the Glasgow club Maxwell FC in 1874, before later joining a more senior club called Parkgrove which was also located in Glasgow. By 1876, his brilliance first became apparent by those involved in the game, and by 1880 his skill and ability was so well recognised, that he was selected to play in an All Glasgow Eleven team which featured the very best players in Scotland at that time.

**Illustration 3: Watson in the All-Glasgow Select Eleven in 1880
(Photo courtesy of the Scottish Football Museum, Glasgow)**

In illustration 3 above, of the All-Glasgow select eleven with Watson featured in the back row, and third from the right, he was, at that time, a member of the Parkgrove Football Club in Glasgow. This demonstrates that he was already making a name for himself as an emerging brilliant footballer in Scotland, in order for him to have been selected for this special Glasgow squad to play against Sheffield and London in 1880.

However, it does not appear that Watson's football career was, from the start, an immediate success. There is even a suggestion that he did not have immediate success, playing football for Parkgrove. We are informed, by an anonymous writer calling himself 'old International' (1896), of some of Watson's involvement in football in Scotland in the 1870s and 1880s. Although the writer only refers to himself as 'Old International', he writes in the first person and from all indications, probably witnessed some of the events he described. Whether Old International was really involved in the game at that level cannot here be ascertained. Some of what he describes, however, seems very plausible and can be corroborated by other contemporary newspaper sources.

According to Old International, in this remarkable account, when Watson first arrived in Scotland from England, he was so familiar with the game of rugby-football, which was the dominant game played at his previous schools, he was not always very sure which rules of the game to follow when he first played for Parkgrove. In one of these early games for example, Watson appeared to momentarily forget the more restrictive rules of the Association game of football, and on more than one occasion, stooped to pick up the ball (Old International, 1896, p. 65). The fact that within a couple of years following this lapse in concentration, he was playing for the prestigious Queen's Park Football Club, speaks volumes of his overall development as a footballer. It also has also to be borne in mind, that Watson was generally an all-rounder in sports being good at high jump and rowing. It was also during this early period of his career at Parkgrove, that Watson got injured, attempting to clear the ball from his goal area by one of his apparent trademark 'huge kicks' but accidently kicked the ground instead which resulted in him dislocating his hip-joint (Old International, 1896, p. 65).

Illustration 4: First Hampden where Queen's Park first played in the late nineteenth century. (Photo courtesy of the Scottish Football Museum, Glasgow)

Illustration 5: A later photo of Second Hampden where Queen's Park also played. This building would have been on part of the first ground where Queen's Park played. Note the terraced buildings in the background overlooking the ground. (Photo courtesy of the Scottish Football Museum, Glasgow)

Illustration 6: Contemporary photo of Hampden Terrace in the vicinity where the first Hamden was located where Queen's Park had their first ground. This street is currently located on what used to be ground where Queen's Park first played. Beyond the houses in the forefront, can be seen a row of buildings which looked down on what used to be the football ground. The terraced buildings were built in the 1870s. (Photo T. Talburt August 2015)

Illustration 7: Location of the original Queen's Park Football Club on Hampden Terrace. (Photo by T. Talburt August 2015)

Illustration 8: Cathkin Park today - This is a small park in Glasgow where Queen's Park Football Club played from 1883 until 1903. (Photo by T. Talburt, August 2015)

Illustration 9: Actual playing field of Cathkin Park today - the Third Lanark Football Club between 1872 and 1967. In the 1880s this was the ground where Watson actually played for Queen's Park. Where the trees are located are the visible remains of the stands or pavilion for spectators. (Photo by T. Talburt, August 2015)

What is even more interesting about this early Parkgrove team was its overall make up of players from different ethnic backgrounds. The goal-keeper, Tommy Martin, was described as being from that land of 'toy and ingenuity' with his flat nose and high cheekbones. He was from Japan and was referred to as being no novice at goal-keeping. In front of Martin was the tall athletic figure of Andrew Watson. He was described as tall though Watson was just under six feet. But the story does not stop here. In the forward or attacking row, was a 'curly-haired son of Africa named Walker' (Old International, 1896, p. 66). Richard McBrearty of the Scottish Football Museum, also supports this point, claiming that both Andrew Watson and Robert Walker, played together for Parkgrove in the Scottish Cup Quarter final game in January 1878 in a game against Vale of Leven, one of the leading teams of the period in Scottish football. Robert Walker also played in the Scottish Cup final in

1876 for Parkgrove and was described at the time as 'darkey Walker' (McBrearty, 2015). Additionally, Robert Walker was also playing football at a very senior level for Parkgrove in the 1870s before Watson joined the club. For example, Walker and Watson both played for Parkgrove in the 1877/1878 season. More interestingly, however, was the fact that Walker played in the Scottish Cup final for the Third Lanark team when they were eventually defeated 2-0 by Queen's Park in 1876. What is fascinating from these accounts is that Robert Walker was, therefore, the world's first Black footballer to actually play in a Scottish cup final, preceding Watson by about five years. Watson would not only play in a cup final a few years later, but would also be part of a winning team. Hence the distinctive point being made here was that Watson was the first Black player to win a national cup competition (McBreaty, 2015).

Illustration 10: Watson and the victorious Scottish national team of 1881 which beat England 6-1 at the Kennington Oval in London. Notice that Watson is sat at the front row because he was the captain of the team. (Photo courtesy of the Scottish Football Museum, Glasgow)

This is the photograph of the team just before their encounter with England, where Watson made his debut appearance and would captain the team. These were the members of the victorious Scotland team which beat England 6-1 in 1881. What is important here was that Watson actually made his debut for the Scottish national team as well as captaining the team to such an overwhelming victory over England. In the same year he helped his club Queen's Park to win the Scottish Cup.

Andrew Watson joined Scotland's most famous amateur club, Queen's Park where, according to Mitchell, his quality as a full back helped to elevate him to the Scottish national team by the end of 1880 (Mitchell, 2013). Watson was officially said to have joined the Queen's Park Football Club on 6 April 1880 from Parkgrove Football Club and eventually left for Liverpool on 1 December 1887 (Robinson, 1920, p. 76).

Watson's Brilliance on the field can be demonstrated by a few of the quotes relating to his style and quality of play during the period. Bone (1890), writing from a personal and first-hand perspective, described him as a 'rare header out who was famed for his fine tackling and neat kicking' (Bone, 1890, p. 44). As far as Bone was concerned, Watson's only fault was that he would often kick the ball out of play when hard pressed by a dashing forward. Today such a practice might be applauded as a precautionary safety first approach to a defender's game. Part of the reason why this approach by Watson might have been regarded as too defensive, was probably due to the nature of the way the game was played during the 1880s and 1890s in Britain. As will be demonstrated later in this study, much of the emphasis pertaining to the tactics or style of the games at that time was based on the power and dominance of the forwards or attacking players.

In terms of Watson's other wider football ability, this was singled out for praise. For example, in the Scottish Cup final in 1881, in which Queen's Park were under a period of sustained pressure from the Dumbarton team, Watson, along with Rowan the goal keeper, and Andrew Holm, were described as having 'displayed ability of the highest order' (Robinson, 1920, p. 116). These two clubs met again in 1882 in April, and Watson was referred to as the player who provided the cross from which Queen's Park scored. Later, both Queen's Park defenders, Andrew Holm and Andrew

Watson were praised for their 'sure kicking, which was the admiration of all' (Robinson, 1920, p. 118).

Despite the points above concerning Watson's great ability, this did not mean he was always without fault of blemish. In one game against Partick Thistle in 1885, when both teams were actually playing in Hampden Park, Scotland, in an English Cup fixture (since the very earliest FA Cup games involved teams from both England and Scotland), Watson's performance, along with a few other team mates, was described as 'not so good' (Robinson, 1920, p. 103). It should be noted, however, that Queen's Park won that game 5-1.

His first football medal was the Glasgow Charity Cup Final in 1880. In 1881 Watson was selected to captain Scotland and, on his debut, led them to a 6-1 win over England. By the end of 1882 he played two more games for Scotland against England and Wales, with both games ending 5-1 in Scotland's favour. In 1882 his club team again won the Scottish Cup final. Precisely because he was an amateur player, it was also at this time that Watson decided to move to England to seek further work as both an engineer and also as a footballer. For this reason, Watson's Scottish national football career came to an abrupt end, as only home-based players for Scottish clubs, were selected for the national Scottish team.

The last quarter of the nineteenth century saw many footballers from Scotland choosing to play in England where they could earn a wage from playing football. This drain of some of Scotland's best players helped to strengthen the English clubs, and up to 1896, the Scottish Football Association refused to include such players in their Scottish national team. This, in effect, meant they were playing professional football in England while the Scottish game was still, until the end of the 1880s, primarily an amateur game. In fact, by the late 1880s, the Scottish FA actually barred sixty eight Scots who were playing professional football south of the border, from playing in their Scottish league which had not yet embraced professionalism. The idea of a professional football league in Scotland was very much considered an immoral practice (Heatley, 2004, p. 26).

As was common among amateur footballers, players were virtually free to play for a number of different clubs in the same season. Therefore, during the middle years of the 1880s, Watson played for a number of different clubs such as the London side Swifts, Brentwood and Pilgrims. His most notable achievement during this period, however, was when he played for, and toured with, the exclusive London amateur football club called Corinthians. One of his main highlights during his time with them was being part of the team's 8-1 'crushing of the then F.A. Cup holders Blackburn Rovers in 1884. He returned to Glasgow occasionally to play for Queen's Park and helped them to win the Scottish Cup in 1886. This was Watson's third Scottish cup-winners medal. He was, as noted earlier in this book, the first Black player to win three national cup winners medals.

Watson's contributions to the development of football in Scotland consisted of much more than just playing the game. Andrew Watson was not only an outstanding footballer, but also served as the secretary of the Parkgrove Football Club and later, the Queen's Park Club. This role involved organising match fixtures, handling correspondences, and aspects of the club's finances. He carried out these functions not only while at Queen's Park, but also earlier in his career when he played for Parkgrove FC in the 1870s. These were no ordinary jobs. By the beginning of the twentieth century, the role of secretary-manager of football clubs had become extremely important. Their roles ranged from signing, selecting and training players, but some were simply administrative clerks who were subservient to their boards of directors (Russell, 1997, p. 88). These managers came to play a crucial role in the public perception of the game. In the early days of the late nineteenth century, the manager was more of a secretary, not necessarily being involved in football tactical decisions.

According to Hutchinson, as the finances and the administration of the clubs grew, so did the responsibilities of the secretary. In the first instance, the club secretaries' job during the 1870s and 1880s was essentially done on a voluntarily basis. Later, secretaries were offered an honorarium or a 'gift' for their services, before eventually becoming full time salaried officials. The other interesting change centred on the relationship between the players and the club officials. Whereas the club secretaries and administrators and their players were seen as equals, by the end of the nineteenth century, this had dramatically changed as players became paid employees, and secretaries and administrators became club bureaucrats (Hutchinson, 1982).

In the 1870s and 1880s when Watson was club secretary of first Park Grove and then Queen's Park, the finances of the football clubs was substantially smaller than what it would become by the end of the nineteenth century. In the mid-1880s for example, Heart of Midlothian ran an account which totalled £3.85. By 1904-1905 English and Scottish football clubs had incomes and expenses of many thousands of pounds and were being run as major business concerns (Hutchinson, 1982, p. 104).

D.D. Bone (1890), writing on Scottish football just a few years after Watson's career ended, regarded him as a significant contributor to the development of football in Glasgow. Watson actually lived and played in the Govan area of Glasgow and, it was from there, that he was instrumental in helping to enhance and develop some aspects of the Parkgrove Football Club. Bone claimed that it was Watson who contributed 'with his ready purse and personal ability… it was in a great measure owing to his (Watson's) interest and energy that the young Parkgrove obtained a proper ground' from which the club could move forward (Bone, 1890, p. 43). Because of Watson's personal wealth, it appears he was able to personally put some of his own money into the running of the club in the years 1878-1880. This certainly seems to suggest that Watson invested some of his wealth into the development of the game in this area of Glasgow. What is significant about this entry by Bone is that Watson appeared to be a significant figure, not only in the playing and development of football in Govant Glasgow where he lived, but also in discussions at the very highest level in these formative years of the game's early development in the city. The suggestion seems to be that Watson invested some of his own money in helping Parkgrove Football Club secure their ground. This would certainly be significant as this would also make Watson the first Black person to financially invest in the development of British football.

Another good example of Watson's influence and overall significance, with regard to the development of football in Scotland and even beyond, could be seen with regard to the proposed Scottish football tour of Canada and USA in the late 1870s. This was meant to serve as a way of exporting the Scottish brand of football in a tour of Canada and the USA. This tour was being organised to help showcase the best of Scottish football, so only the cream of footballers from all the chiefs clubs in Scotland at the time, were being considered for this tournament. According to 'Old International' (1896), Watson was obviously selected as one of these key players but was also a very instrumental personality in these discussions and plans for this event.

Watson's personal influence and significance to the development of football within the city of Glasgow can be seen from the fact, that at the meeting to discuss this proposed tour of Canada and the USA, he was invited to chair the meeting. Watson commented on the difficulties which were likely to arise on such a tour, especially if the players were not able to produce the necessary finances to make the trip possible. He suggested that if financial support was not forth-coming, and the players could not afford to personally contribute to this, the trip should be discouraged. As it turned out, notwithstanding Watson's own personal wealth or status, not many of the other players were able to guarantee such financial commitments. Thus, the planned tour never took place (Old International, 1896, pp. 33-36). What is particularly interesting is that at the period this meeting would have been taking place, Watson would have been no more than twenty three years of age but was already clearly regarded as a successful football player and supporter and possible small time investor in football, as well as an overall significant figure in the development of football in Scotland.

He left Glasgow in the second half of the 1880s to return to England where he played for a team in Liverpool called Bootle

FC which was Everton's main rival. According to Mitchell, this team actually 'offered wages and signing on fees to some of their prominent players,' and there was no doubt that Watson was one of their key attractions. According to Mitchell (2013), if it could be proved that Watson received some finances for playing for this team, this would make Watson the first Black professional footballer and not Arthur Wharton who played in 1889. It also has to be borne in mind, however, whether Watson would have needed to play the game for money, given his personal wealth. Although Watson remained firmly committed to the ideals of the amateur game, there is evidence that amateur players were possibly receiving some form of payment for playing football. Even as late as 1963, we are informed that there were suspicions of illegal payments being made to amateur players, but the main problem was, how to provide proof of these allegations (Mason, 1989, p. 148).

In February 1887 Watson married his second wife, Eliza Kate Tyler as his first wife, Jessie Armour had earlier died in 1882. For the next twenty years Watson worked on ships as an engineer and travelled extensively all over the world including Australia and the USA. By 1892 he became a second engineer. He eventually settled in the London suburb of Kew at 88 Forest Road and died on 8 March 1921. His body is buried at the Richmond Cemetery where his second wife and their daughter are also buried.

Conclusion

This chapter has attempted to do two things. First it has demonstrated the extent to which Andrew Watson could rightly be considered as one of Britain's great pioneering footballers. He was personally involved in the development of football in Glasgow at three different levels. To begin with, he was an amateur player who performed at the highest level possible. Secondly, he played a significant role in football management and administration. Thirdly, he was a financial investor and backer in the development of Parkgrove Football Club, and was involved in very serious discussions about Scottish football in general. The second point the chapter has made, was that the

Andrew Watson story necessarily draws much of its inspiration and background, from two different geographical areas, one in Guyana, where he was born and the other in Glasgow, Scotland, where he played. In this respect, the chapter has shown that the Watson story is closely linked with Guyana, in that at least three generations of his family could claim to have personal connections with this Caribbean country. This was entirely in keeping with a more general pattern of British, and in particular, the presence and influence of Scottish people in Guyana during the second half of the nineteenth century. The chapter has also demonstrated that the city of Glasgow has had, for almost two centuries before Watson's birth, very close involvement with the Caribbean through colonial trade and industry.

CHAPTER FOUR

Watson's Football Achievements in Scotland

No serious discussion on the subject of Watson's contributions to the development of football can take place, without considering two critical factors. The first has to do with an understanding and appreciation of the very origin and development of the modern game of football. This is important, as, during the period when Watson played, the rules and regulations of the game were being established. In Scotland, many of these regulations and guidelines were established or influenced by Queen's Park Football Club, for which Watson was a key player as well as the club's secretary. Therefore, in order to understand how the game developed in Scotland, it is necessary to examine the broader historical context in which the game first developed in England. The second factor which is necessary in attempting to understand and appreciate the significance of Watson, centres on his involvement with Queen's Park Football Club, as well as his inclusion in the Scottish national team. These two concerns are the main objectives of this chapter.

The Origin and Development of Football in Britain

According to Norridge (2008) the game of football, or the kicking of a ball between two teams, probably began in China where there is evidence of a game with rules, competitions and stadiums, during the first millennium A.D (Norridge, 2008, p. 157). Certainly, in the twelfth century in Britain on Shrove Tuesday, it had become fashionable in some towns in England for groups of young men to engage in an annual game of ball. This game consisted of men trying to get hold of a ball and attempt to carry it by force to the place assigned, in order to gain victory. These assigned places or goals could be a considerable distance from each other and, were sometimes even being miles apart (Norridge, 2008, pp. 159-161).

As to the question of when did football begin in Britain, Taylor is probably right. It depends on what we mean by football (Taylor, 2008, p. 19). One of the problems is that the very word 'football' is associated with American football, Australian football, Gaelic football, rugby football, as well as association football (Taylor, 2008, p. 19). Furthermore, very few sports were born or invented at a specific historical moment that could be clearly identified and accepted by all (Taylor, 2008, p. 20).

Despite these debates about the origin of the game, it seems very clear from a number of writers, that the modern game of football has its origins in Britain (Mason, 1989; Harvey, 2005; Taylor, 2008). During the second half of the nineteenth century, as the expansion of the railway network and the improvement in real wages of the working class improved in Britain, these facilitated the further growth or expansion of certain sports especially cricket and horse-racing into new areas of the country (Vamplew, 1988, p. 11). In this context, therefore, a number of different sporting clubs and establishments developed in the nineteenth century which were separate and apart from the game of football, but would later set up football clubs as part of their broader organisations. As a consequence, a number of football clubs formed during this early period, were associated with other sports and business interests completely unconnected with the game of football itself. In some instances, it was initially members of cricket clubs, who were desirous of engaging in a winter sport, which led them to form football clubs. For example, Aston Villa in Birmingham was formed by a group of men connected with the Villa Cross Wesleyan Chapel Cricket Team. West Bromwich Albion, formed in 1879, was established by a group of cricketers called the West Bromwich Strollers who played their games at the Dartmouth Park (Gibbons, 2001, pp. 18, 19).

Once English football clubs started to emerge in the second half of the nineteenth century, another problem arose. This centred on which set of rules the different teams should use to play against each other. During the first half of the nineteenth century there were considerable debates and conflicts regarding the rules by which different clubs would agree to play under. What this meant, was that when teams from different districts or regions decided to play each other, they had to first agree which set of rules the game would be played under. In the course of one season, for example, one team might have to play according to several different sets of rules or codes. This could partially help to explain why, Andrew Watson, initially attempted to pick up the ball and carry it, when he first played for Parkgrove Football Club, having recently arrived in Scotland from England in the mid 1870s, where they played using many different rules. Some degree of confusion was inevitable. Between 1838 and 1863, a number of debates and meetings took place which eventually resulted in the formation of the English Football Association. Cambridge University for example, had several meetings between 1838 and 1842, and in 1846, 1848, 1856, and also in 1863 in attempts to agree and formalise common rules by which teams could play (Taylor, 2008, p. 24). At this period, it was the elite British public schools and universities which were dominating the debates concerning the guidelines under which the game should be played.

Very importantly, however, Taylor also makes the point, that it should not be assumed that it was primarily the public school institutions which laid down the rules or set the overall tone, without some input from other stake-holders, by which this emerging game would come to be recognised and later associated. He claims that by the middle of the nineteenth century, there were popular forms of football being played by non-public school institutions which were 'every bit as sophisticated, rational and influential, as the games played in public school' (Taylor, 2008, p. 26). Some of these teams were associated with pubs, the military and occupational groups and had developed their own rules before the 1863 Association rules were agreed. For example, the Surrey Football Club was founded in 1849 and issued a set of six key rules. Some of these included; no wilful kicking, twenty two a side teams, and how to determine the winner of a game, as being the first team to kick the ball over the goal rope of their opponent's goal (Taylor,

2008, p. 27). For much of the nineteenth century, however, debates concerning the nature of the game, involved a variety of footballing interests, of which the British public schools were very influential.

The main debate regarding the rules of football in the mid nineteenth century, centred essentially upon the issue of the extent to which the handling of the ball should, or should not be allowed. Those institutions like Harrow, Eton and Winchester, preferred a game based more on kicking and dribbling. Marlborough and Rugby, however, preferred a game based more on the handling and carrying of the ball (Goldblatt, 2007, p. 29). The first set of meetings took place to formally establish the Football Association in 1863. One example of the kind of issue which was discussed in these early meetings was that there should be no forward passing of the ball. This, of course, was an attempt to mirror the sport of rugby, which resulted in teams passing the ball to their best dribbler who then charged down the field. He was then backed up by the other players leaving one defender to protect the goal (Norridge, 2008, p. 173). Within a couple of years, the emphasis had changed towards playing the ball with the feet, allowing only the goal keeper to use his hands. Within the context of the public schools, however, football was undergoing significant changes with regard to the rules. Rugby and Eton were amongst the first schools to develop written rules or codes which players had to follow. For example, rules were agreed about when a goal was scored when the ball went through the post, or whether players could still handle the ball, as well as clarity over the off-side rules, the size and shape of the playing field and the duration of matches (Taylor, 2008, p. 23).

October 26 1863 will always be remembered as the day when the English Football Association was formed. It was on this day, that eleven London-based clubs held a meeting at the Freemason's Tavern in Holborn, London to discuss the possibility of forming such as an association (Gibbons, 2001, p. 13). Over the next few years, the wide variety of different rules which were being used by different teams, were generally brought under one set of rules. This helped to bring much greater uniformity to the game of football. For example, handling the ball by outfield players was eventually abolished. Furthermore, goal kicks came into force in 1869, corner kicks in 1872, umpires in 1874, cross bars in 1882, and eleven a-side games became the rule in 1870 as was the addition of a goal keeper (Gibbons, 2001, p. 15).

Historically, the game of football, as it developed in England, was often associated with hooliganism and violence. It appears that from as early as the twelfth century, ferocity and some degree of violence had become critical features of the old mass festival games. In fact, following the drowning of a football player at Derby in 1796, the inquest jury denounced the sport as not only being 'disgraceful to humanity and civilisation' but the Mayor and justices called for such sporting activities to be discontinued (Birley, 1988, p. 23). Nor was this a one-off situation. These games were often violent occasions accompanied with bruises and broken bones. One commentator referred to these ungodly games being played on Sundays, as friendly fights rather than play or recreation (Norridge, 2008, p. 164).

According to Mason (1980), the nature of the football game which was being played even before the last four decades of the nineteenth century was still very rough and accompanied by degrees of violence and physical injuries during matches. In Derby for example, during the nineteenth century, a local game between the two parishes of All Saints and St Peter's Shrove Tuesday Football, had developed into a popular festival involving hundreds of people. However, by the end of the century, this kind of football came to be seen by the authorities, as riots and collective violence and resulted in street football becoming marginalised and criticised (Taylor, 2008, p. 22). During the eighteenth and nineteenth centuries, in little pockets of available spaces, all over the country, more and more football was being played on the streets and local parks or wherever people chose to play. This resulted in local and national authorities attempting to ban such events. The Highways Act of 1835 prohibited the playing of football on the highways with fines of up to 40 shillings being levied on those caught (Mason, 1980, p. 10). As late as the year 1911, of the six hundred and five children brought before the Birmingham Juvenile Court, one hundred and thirty two cases were for those accused of playing football in the streets (Mason, 1980, p. 82). However, nothing, it seems, could prevent the growth of this popular sport.

Certainly, by the nineteenth century, even within the British Parliament, passing references were being made to the game of football. In a debate in the House of Commons on 9 April 1824, pertaining to the Building of Churches Act, to discuss the need for more funds to be allocated for the building of more places of worship, Dr Lushington MP, complained that on Sundays, instead of going to church and engaging in worship, people were playing each other at football, as well as other forms of entertainment (Hansard Parliamentary Debates, 9 April 1824). Similarly in 1838, Parliament debated the need for, and possible consequences of, a closure of a footpath in Notting Hill, as this would lead to more people using a large open area, where, amongst other pleasurable activities, football could be played (Hansard Parliamentary Debates, 2 April 1838). What this demonstrates, is that by the end of the nineteenth century in Britain, the game of football had started to become part and parcel of everyday life.

In Scotland the game of football developed more so than the game of rugby especially in the industrial urban centres like Glasgow. According to Heatley (2004) one of the reasons why the game of football developed and prospered more in Scotland over rugby was due to the fact that 'well-grassed areas were few and far between, especially in the Scottish lowlands' (Heatley, 2004, p. 25). For this reason, football could, and frequently was, improvised anywhere and everywhere. It was, therefore, by the second half of the nineteenth century, becoming an increasingly popular sport.

Scotland's Pioneering Football Team

Andrew Watson's football career was remarkable on a number of accounts, but none more so than the fact that he played for the best national team as well as the two best club teams in Britain. Given the fact that there were no other teams playing at such advanced levels, which could seriously challenge them, during the period when he played, this means Watson was actually playing football for the very best teams in the world. This section looks at the significance of two of these teams for which Watson was a key player; the first was Queen's Park Club Football Club, while the second was the Scotland national team.

We are informed that at eight-thirty on 9 July 1867, thirteen gentlemen met at 3 Eglinton Terrace, in Glasgow, Scotland for the purpose of forming a football club. After a man named Mr Black was called to the chair, a number of measures were voted for, and a football club called Queen's Park was established (Robinson, 1920, p. 10). Among those present at this meeting were the three Smith Brothers. One of them, Robert Smith would also go on to be appointed as Scotland's first national captain (Heatley, 2004, p. 25). From such a humble beginning, this football club would, for the next thirty years, dominate Scottish football.

One of the salient features of Scottish football since the 1860s, which is in stark contrast to the game in England, has been the extent to which only three teams have dominated the history of competitive football north of the border. The nature and significance of Scottish football in the 1870s and 1880s, was as dominated by Queen's Park Football Club, as it is today dominated by Celtic and Rangers. The domination of these two latter clubs can be demonstrated by the fact that between the years 1891 and 1983, excluding the war years of 1914-1918 and 1940-1945, these two clubs won the Scottish Championship sixty four times between them. Furthermore, up to the year 1980, one hundred and twelve Rangers players were capped for Scotland, eighty seven Celtic players and twenty seven from Aberdeen (Moorhouse, 1984, p. 292). What is particularly significant for this study is the fact that when the Queen's Park Club was at its peak in the early to mid-1880s, Andrew Watson was one of their star players.

The significance of Queen's Park Football Club to Scottish and indirectly, British football, cannot be underestimated.

According to Robinson, Queen's Park was responsible for the development of football in Scotland, the Scottish Football Association Code, and ultimately, the very style of play based on the passing-game (Robinson, 1920, p. 6). In keeping with the ethos and nature of the game played in England in the early nineteenth century, the game of football was dominated by those preferring to retain the amateur status of the sport. As a consequence, the aim or purpose of this premier amateur football club in Glasgow was, from the beginning, for the 'amusement and recreation of its members' (Robinson, 1920, 48). It would remain an amateur club, even while most of the other clubs around it, which developed later, eventually became professional, and thus eventually took centre stage in terms of dominating Scottish football. However, although they were an amateur football club, their standard and quality of football was so good, during the last quarter of the nineteenth century, that they were able to compete with, and out-play, most of the Scottish professional teams. It was only in the twentieth century that Queen's Park found they were not able to compete with the professional teams around them, and eventually entered into a downward spiral of decline as a significant force in Scottish football.

From its establishment in 1867, Queen's Park led the way in terms of the development of Scottish football in a number of different ways. The club was very instrumental in establishing the main rules or legislations of the game played in Scotland (Robinson, 1920, pp. 47-56). It was Queen's Park which played a critical role in helping to decide the rule regarding the throw-ins, which, in the end, were to be taken in any direction. They were also instrumental in influencing the rule regarding the half-time changing of ends, regardless of the score. In fact, Murray goes much further than Robinson, by declaring that it was Queen's Park who founded the Scottish game in 1867 and dominated it, for the better part of the next twenty years even after the establishment of Rangers in 1872 and Celtic in 1887 (Murray, 1984, p. 10).

Illustraton 11: The Queen's Park football team of 1880/1881 with Andrew Watson pictured second from the left in the back row. (Photo courtesy of the Scottish Football Museum, Glasgow)

Queen's Park Football Club not only helped to set the main rules governing the sport in Scotland, they were also one of the oldest football clubs in the world. They were also undeniably, the most dominant football team in Scotland. From their inception in 1867 until 1875, in all the games Queen's Park played, no team was ever able score a goal against them. The first goal they conceded, came in a match with Vale of Leven by a player named R. Paton, just before half-time in a game played in 1875 (Robinson, 1920, p. 56). What was even more remarkable, given that there were now more teams competing in Scottish football, Queen's Park never lost a match until 1876 (Robinson, 1920, p. 58). During the early 1880s this was the period when Queen's Park Football Club 'stood at its apogee as a force in football' (Robinson, 1920, p. 123). Robinson's claim is certainly no exaggeration. Were it not for the care given to Association

Football in Scotland by Queen's Park, the game would never have taken the place it has in the world of sport, nor would Scotland stand where it does, as the 'nursery and home of football as at present played in all parts of the world' (Robinson, 1920, p.3). This almost immodest statement could fittingly be used with regard to this club, and, very few could seriously argue otherwise.

Part of the reason for their success on the field stemmed from their particular or unique style of play. The main method adopted and perfected by the Queen's Park Club was based on the transference or the passing of the ball, accompanied by strong backing up, which were those qualities and skills which got the best out of the team. This style of football, based on passing the ball rather than focusing exclusively on individual dribbling, was referred to as combination style and was the chief characteristic of the Queen's Park play' (Robinson, 1920, p. 27). This was Scotland's unique gift to the rest of the football world. It was, however, the very opposite approach to that style of play practised in England. In fact, according to Goldblatt, in the 1860s and 1870s, the passing of the ball was only considered as a measure of last resort and indicated failure and even dishonour (Goldblatt, 2007, p. 35). By the early 1880s Queen's Park was experimenting with the playing of three half-backs and were soon joined by many other leading teams. What this meant was that they employed a centre-half to play between the two wide defenders, thus giving them more strength in defence.

The English teams, on the other hand, based their game on the individual skill and strength of their forwards. Queen's Park, and subsequently, other Scottish teams, used a team approach, passing the ball between their players rather than focusing primarily on their forwards and an approach based on attacking football. This is why Robinson would declare that Scottish football, as played by Queen's Park had become a powerful force in the land, but more importantly, an international example (Robinson, 1920, p. 4). This was the particular skill which Queen's Park gave to England and indirectly to the rest of the world. It was from the middle of the 1870s and throughout the 1880s that the club really started to develop, and ultimately, export this approach. Robinson informs us that Queen's Park never neglected to engage in practice and training. It was during these training sessions, that techniques in passing and dribbling were developed (Robinson, 1920, p. 27). Much of the football played in Britain, especially in England, up the late 1880s was based on the physical size and strength in numbers of the forward players. Most teams played with 8 forwards and 2 defenders with a 1-1-8 formation.

What is important to note here, was that Andrew Watson was a key player for the top team in Scotland, which based their football on this passing or combination style. Watson was described as one of the two important men who joined the Queen's Park Club in 1880. He joined Queen's Park on 6 April 1880 and left for Liverpool on 1 December 1887 (Robinson, 1920, p. 76). At the very period when Queen's Park was dominating Scottish football, due in part to their particular method of play, Watson was an integral member of the team. He would have been very conversant with this approach. If it is true that Queen's Park and other Scottish clubs thereafter, developed and were later responsible for helping to export of this style of football to the rest of England, then surely Watson should be regarded as part of this success story.

By the time Andrew Watson started playing football at a senior level in Scotland, first for Maxwell FC and then Parkgrove, the Scottish football clubs were having similar debates and controversies about the nature of their game. It was in this context that Queen's Park emerged as the principle team in Scotland which, during the 1870s and 1880s, laid the foundation for much of Scottish football, in terms of not only the rules of the game, but ultimately, the very style of playing. As will become clearer in this chapter, Queen's Park became the dominant team in Scotland, which was primarily responsible for the development of the modern game of football, which would be subsequently exported to England. Watson was, therefore, playing for them at a critical period when they were establishing the foundations of the rules as well as the unique style of football which was unmistakably Scottish.

Not only were Queen's Park crucial in the development of this style of football, they were, by far, the very best team in Scotland. Such was their dominance in Scottish football, that when the first officially recognised international match between England and Scotland occurred in 30 November 1872 at the Hamilton Crescent Partick, all eleven players for Scotland were from the Queen's Park Football Club. The England team on the other hand, had been drawn from players representing a number of different English clubs. Although this was really a national club against a country, the game ended even with neither side being able to score. In the first match played between these two, the Scottish formation was 2-3-5 while England's team played with a 1-1-8 formation. This demonstrated the different styles being adopted by the two teams. The approached used by the England team, placed more emphasis on attacking, whereas the Scottish team played with two defenders, which, at the time, was considered revolutionary.

This strong dominance by Queen' park was not a one-off. A few years, later when Scotland played England in 1882, seven of the players were from the Queen's Park Club, one of these was, of course, Andrew Watson. Queen's Park Football Club was regarded as the most prestigious and developed amateur club and this was the club for which Watson made thirty six appearances between 1880 and 1887. The main point being made in this section of the study is that this style of football was revolutionary and at the forefront of this approach in the 1880s was Andrew Watson, who was a very key senior player at the club and one of the proponents of this combination-style of football being played in Scotland.

Watson's International Football Career

As the game of football started to become increasingly popular, not only were club matches being played everywhere, but international encounters also developed. C.A. Allcock was the first secretary of the English FA as well as one of the chief instigators of the first ever international football match. The first match took place on 30 November 1872 and was watched by about 4000 spectators. As expected, the bulk of the England team consisted of university students, one of whom, C.J. Ottaway, from Oxford University, was the captain. This was, as we have already mentioned, a draw. Although the game ended in a 0-0 draw, one of its main effects was to publicly display the virtues of the passing game which Queen's Park had virtually mastered. In terms of the style of play, the Queen's Park club had introduced the short passing game instead of the game based on dribbling forward with their team mates behind them as back-up. It also galvanised the popularity of the game in Scotland resulting in the establishment of the Scottish FA in 1873 (Norridge, 2008, p. 176).

In the next international encounter, which occurred on 8 March 1873 at London's Kennington Oval, England emerged as victors by 4 goals to 2. It should be mentioned here, that England adopted the Scottish approach of using a 2-3-5 formation. From then on, it seemed that these international matches became an annual event. The next match was played in 1874 in Partick, Scotland which was won by the Scottish team 2-1. The following year the game was played in England with C.A. Alcock, captaining the England team. This ended in a 2-2 draw. The years 1876, 1877 and 1878 saw England suffer defeats to the Scottish team. In the 1880s although England had many players to call upon from which to select their team, they persisted in relying largely upon a narrow range of players from the regions in and around London.

Watson's debut against England on 12 March 1881 at the Surrey Cricket Ground, the Oval, Kennington, was truly remarkable event. Eight thousand five hundred people gathered to watch this game. This was one of the largest crowds gathered to watch a football game in England. Watson was also playing with four other team mates from Queen's Park and so it is no wonder that they were easily able to beat England by 6-1. In the second game, played a few days later

Illustration 12: Watson pictured here with Scottish national team which played Wales in Wrexham in 1881. (Photo courtesy of the Scottish Football Museum, Glasgow)

in Wrexham, Wales, Watson played and helped Scotland to a 5-1 victory. This game was played on 14 March 1881 in front of a crowd of one thousand five hundred people.

A year later in the return game between Scotland and England on 11 March 1882, some fifteen thousand people watched as Scotland beat England 5-1. There were ten thousand people in the ground and another five thousand watching from the slopes outside. This game was played at Hampden Park Hampden Terrace in Glasgow, Lanarkshire. Andrew Watson's club team mate Charles Campbell, captained the national team to a 5-1 win over England. In this game there were seven Queen's Park players in the national team. In this game Scotland played using a 2-2-6 formation.

Scotland's dominance in international games with England can be clearly seen from an examination of the games played in the 1870s and 1880s. Scotland won nine out of the eleven of the international encounters with England after 1872. More specifically, of the sixteen matches played between England and Scotland during the period 1872 and 1887, England had only won twice and the teams had drawn four times. In the other ten games Scotland had beaten England. This clearly demonstrates the extent of the Scottish dominance in international football matches against England during this period.

The key point to note from these friendly international games was that Scotland played using the same tactical approach, as the Queen's Park team. It should come as no surprise, therefore, that the national team was able to apply the same general approach. The England team, by contrast, was selected from players representing a wide range of different clubs. More significantly, however, these England players were not as comfortable playing this style of football. Much this was, as will be explained more in chapter six, was an attitudinal issue about individualism rather than a team approach, and possibly, also related to the way in which the game originated and developed in England.

Watson also played for the Scottish national team which was arguably the best national team in the world at that time. After having joined Queen's Park in 1880, within a year, Watson's very impressive performances were rewarded when he was appointed captain of the Scottish national team in March 1881. Even though his international career was very short and consisted of three appearances between 1881 and 1882, this was particularly momentous. Playing for the Scottish national team was a significant achievement in itself, but being made captain of the team speaks volumes of Watson's ability. In all three games, the main reason for Scotland's victories was their combination play based on individual dribbling along-side organised team play, based on the short passing game. Watson was obviously familiar with this style of play and was also very good at it. The fact that Watson played for the very top club team in Scotland as well as the national team suggests he was an exceptional player. During the 1880s Watson was one of the very best defenders in the country playing for the very best club team in Scotland (if not in Britain) at the time (Queen's Park) as well as the Scottish national team itself. This level of Scottish dominance did not go unnoticed in England, and this is why

Corinthians of London, which went on to become the very best amateur club in Britain, even into the early twentieth century, also sought the services of Watson.

Conclusion

What this chapter has shown is that Watson played for two of the very best teams in Scotland during the 1880s. Both teams played the game according to the same general ethos and style based on the passing or combination approach. This called for greater emphasis on team play rather than individual skills. It was no surprise, therefore, that many of the players on the Scottish national team, were from the Queen's Park Club. In this way, they were able to simply continue playing the kind of club football for their national team. Andrew Watson was an integral member of both teams, and this is the reason for examining the nature of these two teams. During the 1880s this new revolutionary style of football was very much linked with Queen's Park and the Scottish national team. This also helps to explain why footballers from Scotland, including Watson, were in such demand by other football clubs in England. This Scottish influence in the development of the modern game of football was their main gift to England. The next chapter, therefore, discusses the origin and development of the game in England as a result of the influence of Scottish-players, including Watson, who moved south of the border to play football.

CHAPTER FIVE

The Scottish Black Professor in England

This chapter focuses on the ways in which Scotland contributed to the general development of football in Britain in the 1870s, through to the end of the nineteenth century. In doing so, it also assesses the specific role of Watson, as part of the wave of Scottish-based footballers, who travelled south of the border to ply their trade in England and thereby ended up teaching, influencing and ultimately, helping to modernise how those teams subsequently came to play football. This was, as the chapter makes clear, particularly prevalent in the north of England, where the dominance of football clubs from the north of the country as well as Midlands were apparent.

Scotland's contributions to the development of the modern game of football in Britain during the period 1870s to the 1890s is important for our purposes because this was the period when hundreds of Scottish-based players moved south of the border to play in England for wages. This great wave of players had a significant impact on the way the game would eventually come to be played in England. These decades were also important because they corresponded with a time in Glasgow's history which was accompanied not only by spectacular economic growth and development (Moorhouse, 1984, pp. 294, 295), but also by the growth in popularity of football among its working classes.

In fact, in Giulianotti and Robertson's (2009) study on globalisation and football, the 1870s-1920s was considered a critical period in the development and spread of football across Europe and the rest of the world. They contend that the game of football has been a highly important aspect of the globalisation process which took place over five phases stretching from the fifteenth to the twenty-first century. The first phase covered the period from the fifteenth to the nineteenth century where various forms of football, or a game involving the kicking of a ball between two teams or groups, took place in different parts of the world (Giulianotti and Robertson, 2009, pp.5-7). The second phase covered the period of the early nineteenth century to 1870, and was characterised by the development of many aspects of the modern game influenced by the 'social elites' in Britain, who established the bulk of the governing rules of the game (Giulianotti and Robertson, 2009, p. 6). The third phase covered the period from 1870 to the 1920s, while the fourth phase covered the period from the 1920s to the late 1960s in what the writers describe as the 'struggle for hegemony,' where different countries competed for global dominance of the game in terms of rules, commercial influence and the power and influence of their national players who were regarded as national heroes (Giulianotti and Robertson, 2009, p. 15). The fifth period covered the years from the 1960s through to the 2000s.

Eric Dunning also identified four stages in the development of the modern game of football. Dunning's first stage was during the fourteenth to the eighteenth centuries in which football existed in a fairly simple, wild and unruly folk games which varied considerably from place to place (Taylor, 2008, p. 20). Dunning's second stage covered the specific period from 1750-1840 and involved the 'adoption and adaptation' by the public schools of the folk game. The third stage involved the writing of the formal rules of the game by the middle of the nineteenth century. The final stage from 1850-1890 focused on the period when the game developed a mass appeal and where, main written rules of the association football were established (Taylor, 2008, pp. 20, 21).

It is, however, Giulianotti's third period from the 1870s and corresponding periods in Dunning's third and fourth stages in the second half of the nineteenth century, which is significant for this study. This was the period when football was becoming embedded within the popular cultures of Europe and South America, and in the 'Europeanised' parts of Africa, Asia and North America (Giulianotti and Robertson, 2009, p. 7). It is interesting to note, therefore, that at the very time when the sport was being developed and beginning to emerge on the world scene from the 1870s and 1880s, the Scottish influence on the development and modernisation of football, was at its peak. It is remarkable, then, that Andrew Watson featured significantly during this phase in the development of British football history as one of Britain's best players.

Taylor makes the point that the Industrial Revolution which took place in Britain from the second half of the eighteenth century did not diminish the level of public interest in the game. For example, he cites particular cases in Oxfordshire and Lancashire where, factory production and urbanisation were extremely pronounced, yet the traditional football festivals survived well into the nineteenth century (Taylor, 2008, p. 25). One factor which contributed to the development and spread of football, especially among the working classes in Britain, was the increase in real wages which occurred during the last quarter of the nineteenth century. This increase was brought about largely because of the impact of industrialisation and its accompanying urbanisation. It is estimated that family incomes increased by about 30% during this period (Goldblatt, 2007, p. 52). Accompanying these changes in family and personal fortunes, was the growing popularity of half-day holidays on Saturdays, which helped to ensure that an ever increasing crowd support was able to attend football matches.

The increasing popularity of football was accompanied by significant changes in the way the game was played. It was particularly within this context that the influence of Scottish players would affect the development of the game in England. Until the early 1880s, the focus of the annual Cup competitions in England was dominated by the 'amateur gentlemen' primarily from the south of the country (Walvin 1994b. p. 73). However, partly as a result of Scottish players moving south of the border to play in the northern parts of England, bringing with them much greater skills and a team-approach to the game, they began to influence the way the game was played. Mason also commented on the fact that the borrowing of players from other clubs for important matches became increasingly popular by the end of the 1870s. Such activities were considered by some to be against the spirit of the game, especially when the 'imported professors' came from north of the border (Mason, 1980, pp. 70, 71). This Scottish influence within English football teams in the north of the country helped many of them to change the way they played the game.

That it was the country of Scotland, which gave the modern game of football to the rest of the world, can hardly be doubted. Even though we have already examined the significance of Queen's Park Football Club, earlier in the nineteenth century, the first ever football club was formed in Edinburgh in 1824. It was called the Football Club of Edinburgh. It was formed by a seventeen year old law student named John Hunt. In keeping with the nature of football played in Britain at that time, the team was made up of members from professional backgrounds such as doctors and accountants. Although this was a very different kind of football, in the sense that it was a very rough game with probably more kicking of shins than kicking of the ball, along with pushing and shoving, but never the less, this was certainly recognised as the very first football club team in the world and was finally disbanded in 1841 (Mclean, 2014).

Scotland influenced football in England in two other inter-related ways; first through the style of play and secondly, through their importation of Scottish footballers in great numbers into English clubs primarily in the north of the country. For much of the two decades from 1870, football was essentially an amateur game played by gentlemen from very privileged socio-economic backgrounds. By the 1890s in both Scotland and England, the game had become professional. One of the features of the style of football played especially by the players from the elite universities and schools in the south of England was their emphasis on individual dribbling skills as opposed to the passing of the ball. As Walvin points out, the whole emphasis of the games during that period was to attack, hence most of the players were forwards and dribbling was the norm (Walvin, 1994b, p. 74). It was in this particular respect that Scotland changed the way the game was played in England. This, as we saw in the previous chapter, was primarily brought about by Scotland's premiere amateur club, Queen's Park, which as we have seen, had been formed in 1867. Unlike the gentlemen footballers of Eton, Harrow and Rugby, the emphasis and general style of football in Scotland was based on a combination of passing as well as dribbling with a strong desire and ambition to play and win as one team.

One description of the dribbling game was;

> The good dribbler retained the ball as long as possible, especially if he combined speed with control. Long runs were the thing of the day. There was, however, a system of backing up, that of a player who followed up the dribbler, ready to receive the ball if it came to him, or to hustle and ward off any interference by the opposing forwards or back (Taylor, 2008, p. 87).

The fact was that the typical English style of play up to the 1890s was based on eight attacking players with one defender and one mid-field player adopting a 1-1-8 formation. The typical English approach was based on the forward players dribbling their way through to the goal. Queen's Park and the Scottish national team, however, had a different system based on 2-2-6 formation or sometimes a 2-3-5 formation. This would still be considered very attacking by today's standards. However, Queen's Park's approach at least, had two definite defenders and sometimes three to check the advance of the opposing attackers. It was only by the end of the 1890s that English clubs, primarily in the north of the country, began to change their style and formations in line with this Scottish approach. They were able to adopt this style by engaging the services of Scottish-based players, or the 'Scottish Professors.' This is what helped to make the Scottish club teams and their national team so strong and virtually unbeatable. Commenting on the international game between England and Scotland in 1878, Gibbons' sub-heading aptly described it in the following words, 'The Scots Run England Ragged' (Gibbons, 2001, p. 50). In the game between the two played in 1881, Gibbons summed up England's defeat in three words, 'England are Humiliated' (Gibbons, 2001, p.61). It was primarily because of their style and approach to the game, which explained why the Scottish teams were so strong and became the envy of the English.

Mason informs us that the Scots, particularly those connected to the Queen's Park Football Club, appeared to have pioneered the passing game in the 1870s. When, for example, Queen's Park visited Aston Villa in 1881 (by which time Watson, was a player at the club) they were described as having played as one team. Mason, quoting from the *Birmingham Daily Mail*, 21 October 1881 which commented on the approach by Queen's Park, said 'every player being in his place at the right moment. The backs and half-back played splendidly...the dribbling being close and good and passing wonderfully accurate, while no trace of selfishness was visible in any one of them' (Mason, 1980, p. 208). This had a revolutionary and modernising impact on the way the game would be played thereafter by the English clubs. By the late 1880s Preston North End was arguably the best football team in England, and had been influenced, in part, by the importation of Scottish players who used this combination football incorporating dribbling and passing. Preston North End's dominance of the English game can be seen with reference to the fact that in March 1887, to commemorate Queen Victoria's 50 years on throne, they were invited to play the elite amateur team Corinthians of London as part of a Festival of Football at the Kennington Oval in London in which both teams played to 1-1 draw (Vasili, 1998, p. 66). Preston North End was not only the first English league champions in the first season 1888-1889, with Aston Villa finishing second, they also achieved the league and cup double. What was truly remarkable about this English team, was that they went through the entire league season undefeated and did not concede a goal within the FA Cup competition (Heatley, 2004, p. 22). As mentioned earlier in this study, in chapter two, this was one of the teams Arthur Wharton played for, which also highlights the fact that he was playing for one of the best football teams in Britain at that time.

Over the next few years, Aston Villa and Sunderland, who were both dominant in the 1890s could, according to Mason, similarly attribute much of their success to the importation of Scottish players who were particularly skilled in the passing game (Mason, 1980, p. 214). Through this way, Scottish players were able to join and influence, and, in some cases teach the English how to play the passing game. For this reason, the Scots were referred to as the 'professors' and Watson, could thereby qualify as the 'Black Scottish professor' by virtue of the fact that he too, came to England to play for English clubs.

The number of Scottish players taking part in the game in England was also fairly significant. It was the English clubs in the north of the country, which were also less influenced by the social elitism often associated with the leading public schools and universities in the southern half of the country, which led the way in this modernising and revolutionary aspect of the game. In the English clubs from the north of the country, where the game was more advanced than in the south of England, is where it became clearly evident that more teams were keen to 'import' Scottish players. In 1885 for example, there were fifty eight Scottish footballers playing for English clubs and fifty seven of them played for teams in Lancashire 'the hotbed of professional football' at that time (Vasili, 1998, p. 56). In 1884 and 1885 Queen's Park Football Club had reached the finals of the English FA Cup where they were beaten both times by Preston North End. What is worthy of note is the fact that Preston North End beat them 3-0 with the 'help of half a dozen expatriate Scots' (Vasili, 1998, p. 60). More importantly, within a few years, a number of other English clubs were playing the passing game which had been introduced to them from Scotland. The fact that Preston North End was able to do so was precisely because they had a team composed mainly of Scottish players.

In 1883 Blackburn Olympic from the North of the country beat the Old Etonians in the FA Cup final to become the first team from the north to do so. Part of their secret rested on the formation and training they put in to their game which was in stark contrast to the Eton team who assumed they only needed to turn up in order to win. This was the last time that a southern amateur team ever won the FA Cup. As Norridge makes clear, the working class clubs from the industrial north and the midlands of England had begun to transform and dominate British football (Norridge, 2008, pp. 179-181). It was becoming obvious for those who wished to see, that English football was changing, and that much of this change was coming from these working class industrial towns in the north of England. In 1870 Charles Alcock became Honorary Secretary of the FA and in 1871 proposed a knock out completion for its member clubs. This is what became the FA Cup and the first FA Cup competition was held in 1872, and was won by the old Harrovian side called the Wanderers who beat the Royal Engineers at the Oval in front of a crowd of 2000 (Norridge, 2008 p. 175). Within a few years, however, it would be the clubs from the north of the country which would dominate this competition.

The pattern of English teams from the north of the country, using a large number of Scottish players, became a significant feature of English football at this time. The first eleven players to play for Liverpool were all Scots (Murray, 1984, p. 6). Similarly, the Everton team which won the league title in 1890-91 had four outstanding Scottish players in their team. For the following two seasons, the league was won by a Sunderland team which had ten Scottish players and even the one Englishman, Tom Porteous, had himself, apparently joined from a Scottish club (Golesworthy, 1972, pp. 19-27). Aston Villa was the other team which dominated the English football League championship in the 1890s and also had five Scottish players in the first team. The Tottenham Hotspur Team based in North London which achieved promotion from the second Division at the beginning of the twentieth century, consisted of eleven northern players, that is, players from either Scotland or from the north of the England (Heatley, 2004, p. 25). In fact, Birley makes this point even clearer, by pointing out that when Tottenham won the FA Cup in 1901, the team consisted of three northerners, two Welshmen, an Irishman and no fewer than five Scots (Birley, 1995, p. 42). The Chelsea Football Club which was established in 1905 had a former Glasgow Rangers player as manager and 'a lot of imported Scottish players' (Birley, 1995, p. 231).

Such was the dominance of Scottish players in the teams from the north of England, that between 1895 and 1914,

Scotland was never able to field an international eleven, based on players who played in their own Scottish League. In fact, by 1928 when Scotland played England at Wembley only three of the Scottish players in the starting eleven were playing for Scottish teams. The others were playing mainly for teams in the north of the country. For the England team, there were only two players who actually played for teams in the south of the country. This again helps to demonstrate the extent to which teams in the north and midlands of the country still dominated the game well into the 1920s.

At first, the approach by Scotland to first infiltrate the English game with their numerous players, and then change the style of play, was not always appreciated. For example, when Scotland beat England in 1884 one English reporter complained about the formation of three defenders that the Scottish team used which 'checked all dribbling and scientific play' (Mason, 1980, p. 210). Similarly, the importation of Scotsmen to play in the English clubs created some hostilities and negative comments. In Lancashire by the 1880s, they had a number of imported players, playing for local clubs 'not to mention actual paid men', which the football Association tried to ban from cup ties in 1882 but this initiative failed (Mason, 1980, p. 71).

The problem was that a tide of professionalism, using Scottish players, was sweeping down into England and it would prove difficult to stop. As one J.J. Lang was said to have remarked, 'he hadn't crossed the border to play for nothing' (Goldblatt, 2007, p. 46). The English FA grudgingly accepted or conceded defeat in 1885 but still tried to cling to their social class bias, which had a strong preference in favour of amateur football, by ensuring that when the first professional player played for England, he wore a blue coloured shirt while the rest of the team played in white (Goldblatt, 2007, p. 47).

During the formative years of the 1860s and 1870s when the game in Britain was developing, it was, of course, the teams from the southern half of the country which dominated the early FA Cup competitions. For example, during the 1870s the FA Cup finalists consisted of teams made up of public school old boys, university students, or military teams based in the south of England. In 1882, however, the Old Etonians faced a different kind of team. This was Blackburn Rovers, a team from the north of the country whose players were from working class backgrounds (Goldblatt, 2007, p. 37). By 1886, following the emergence and development of the professional teams in England, no amateur team would ever make the final of the FA Cup again. This, with very few exceptions, would really mark the beginning of the end of high quality amateur football clubs, in preference for professional teams.

In London and the south of England there was initially fierce resistance to professional players and this resulted in the English Football League which was formed in 1863, being comprised essentially of teams from the midlands and the north. For example, in the 1892-1893 English football season, of the twenty eight clubs in Divisions one and two, ten were in Lancashire, six in Staffordshire, two each in Warwickshire, Yorkshire, Lincolnshire, Cheshire, and Nottinghamshire and one each in Durham and Derbyshire. This shows the extent to which the teams from the south of the country were not very well represented in the football league.

The dominance of northern clubs, many of which were made up of Scottish players or, players adopting the Scottish approach, can also be seen from the fact that between 1883 and 1915, it was primarily clubs from the north and the midlands of England which dominated the FA Cup competitions. Clubs from these regions of England won the FA Cup twenty one times (Walvin, 1994b, p. 78). Similarly when the English Football League was formed in 1888 with twelve founding clubs, all of them were from the north and midlands of England (Walvin, 1994b, p. 86). As mentioned earlier, even several years later when an English Second Division was set up, of these twenty eight teams now playing in the English professional league, none of them came from the south of the country. Such was the dominance of the north over the south in terms of football power and decision making, that even the very English Football League's main offices were not located in London, but in Preston and its senior administrative staff were predominantly drawn from Lancashire which was a rarity for a national head institution (Goldblatt, 2007, p. 58).

It was partly because so many Scots were going to play south of the border, and thereby making it impossible for the Scottish national team to field a good international team, that it was decided to form their own Scottish league. As Heatley pointed out, since Scotland refused to play the 'exiles' and inevitably suffered defeat at the hands of the English in international matches, especially the one in 1893 where they lost 5-3, it was decided to introduce professionalism in Scotland (Heatley, 2004, p. 27).

Even with regard to the formation of the English Football League, it was a Scotsman who was instrumental. As Heatley has intimated, it is a little far-fetched, but the founder of the English League was not only Scottish, but a man who never played a first class game of football (Heatley, 2004, p. 22). William McGregor was a draper who had come to live in Birmingham where he set up his small business. He was also a member of the board of Aston Villa and was considered to be one of the key figures in the development of the Aston Villa Football Club in 1874. McGregor was also the recognised key official and founder of the English League in 1888. Football clubs' revenues were based on them having a good cup run and any early exit would result in them making less money. Furthermore, playing too many replays resulted in friendly fixtures being postponed, which led to spectators being disappointed and disillusioned. To avoid this problem, McGregor suggested the formation of a league where fixtures could be properly organised to facilitate its member clubs. Thus, in 1888, the English Football League was formed.

As British people travelled to distant parts of the world to settle or engage in international trade, they took the game of football with them. In this respect too, there were significant Scottish influences. For example, by the end of nineteenth century some thirty thousand British nationals had settled in Buenos Aires. A number of schools were established and the playing of football was a major component of the schools' curricula. A Scots man named Alexander Watson Hutton had established one such school in Argentina, and by 1893, had become the president of the Argentinean Football Association. His school, the English High School, was an early winner of the local championship (Garland and Rowe, 2001, p. 27).

In the last quarter of the nineteenth century, Scotland's contribution to the development of football in Britain and subsequently the world was immense, especially when taken into consideration the relatively small size of the country compared to England. They influenced the way the game was played by moving from Scotland to play for English clubs and helped to transform the style of play. Scotland was involved in the first international game in 1872 with England, the first organised women's game which was played in Inverness in 1888, and also the first penalty kick in an official match which took place at Airdrieonian in 1891 (Goldblatt, 2007, p. 68).

Andrew Watson, along with hundreds of other Scottish Professors was instrumental in helping to transform the modern game of football in Britain. Watson was involved at two levels. First he played for the Queen's Park Club and Scotland where this style had been developed and pioneered. Secondly, he travelled south of the border and played for a number of clubs in the north and south of England. Because Queen's Park, obviously took part in competitions involving teams from England up to the 1880s, this meant that Watson was therefore involved in such games where the team could almost show case this style of football to top English teams. At a more senior level, Watson was also able to be part of this for the three times he played for Scotland. Here, Scotland was able to demonstrate the value of this modern and revolutionary approach in their games against England and Wales during the period 1881-1882. Watson was an integral part of these winning teams.

Watson was probably the world's first 'Black football professor' in the sense that he came to England and played for a number of English clubs where this combination style of football was being introduced or developed. Here too, he was playing for some of the top teams at the time and helping to contribute to this same Scottish style of football. No doubt his greatest accomplishment as a Black football professor occurred when he joined the Corinthians Football Club. As we will see in the next chapter, their very origin and existence was based on the need to develop this modernising approach and show case it all over Britain and, indeed to the rest of the world.

Conclusion

It is clear that Scotland was very instrumental in the development of the modern game of football in England. Whilst this is probably generally known and appreciated by a few people and sports historians, what is often not emphasised is the fact that Andrew Watson could be considered as one of these players from Scotland who was involved in this process. By playing for at least four different English clubs, Watson would certainly have contributed to this new revolutionary and modernising approach. Watson, like so many players based in Scotland, came to England and contributed to the style of football which would later be adopted by these English clubs. Many of these clubs in turn would dominate the English leagues and the FA Cup competition primarily because of their style of play which had been adopted from Scotland. It should come as no surprise that the Corinthians Club, would seek to acquire his services as they attempted to adopt this style. They wanted him not only for his footballing abilities, but, notwithstanding his ethnicity, also his social standing as a fine gentleman with good educational background, wealth and his commitment amateurism. These issues, pertaining to social elitism in British football, form the basis of the next chapter.

CHAPTER SIX

A Footballer and a Gentleman

Andrew Watson was not only an excellent footballer who played for two of Scotland's top teams, but, because of his education and schooling in three of Britain's finest institutions, as well as his enormous wealth, he was treated like a member of Britain's social elite in the late nineteenth century. This chapter, therefore, draws on this broader theme of a strong and important link between Victorian elitism and sports, although particular emphasis is given to football. This was an absolutely crucial factor in the conflicts of interests pertaining to the origin, development and nature of the modern game of football in Britain during the 1870s and 1880s. Notwithstanding his ethnicity or Blackness, it was precisely because of Watson's social background, that he was able to fit into the team ethos, spirit and philosophy of one of Britain's best and also socially elitist football clubs called Corinthians. For Watson to have been selected for such a team, at that time, was a clear demonstration of his footballing ability as well as his personality and social standing.

Victorian Elitist Values and Sports

One of the most physically striking and significant features of Victorian Britain was the rapid growth and spread of urbanisation. Figures by Asa Briggs show that when Queen Victoria came to the throne in 1837, there were only five cities in England and Wales outside of London, with a population of more than one hundred thousand, whilst in 1800 there were none. By 1891 there were twenty three cities with populations of more than one hundred thousand. In Glasgow, just like London, the city had a huge pull on the population. For example, in 1801 only 5.1% of the Scottish population lived in Glasgow, but by 1851 this figure was 11.5% and 19.4% in 1891 (Briggs, 1968, p. 59).

With this changing shift towards urbanisation, came new social conflicts, largely between those who welcomed these accompanying variations and those who did not. This was particularly evident in the emergent modernising game of football, as well as within sports more generally. Increasingly throughout the nineteenth century, the type of sports people engaged in, and they manner in which they were played, became important signals of a person's social standing in Britain. According to Huggins (2004), the Victorian sporting experience was largely a product and a reflection of social class. Class as well as gender, respectability and the division between urban and rural settings, were major factors in determining the nature of sport and leisure activities (Huggins, 2004). By the middle of the nineteenth century in Britain, yachting, shooting, hunting, racing, cricket and rowing were the key sports associated with prestige, power and influence. The typical image was characterised by the Victorian gentleman striving for sportsmanship, fair play, fellowship and discipline (Huggins, 2004, p. 21). Many members of the aristocracy indulged in sport and, during the nineteenth century, were greatly admired and looked up to as true sportsmen with 'less vice, who could run horses, play games honestly, and bet for fun' (Huggins, 2004, p. 22). According to Huggins by 1867 some ninety thousand middle-class families were enjoying incomes of £300 a year or more, and were also finding that their working hours were shortening, thus enabling them to spend more time in sporting leisure (Huggins, 2004, p. 30).

Thomas (1985) also supported this general point, and in his attempt to summarise or define the meaning of Victorianism, suggested three key features; the first was the high-mindedness achieved through Christian education, secondly domesticity within a close family structure, and thirdly, amateurism which was opposed to professionalism (Thomas, 1985, p. 285). The period of the nineteenth century, Thomas argued, was noted for developing professional and technical brilliance within the education system, and at the same time, for ensuring the continuation of a narrow traditional curriculum which would focus on preserving these values (Thomas, 1985, pp. 285-286).

The late nineteenth century represented a period of transition or a cultural crossroads between those wishing to preserve the old order, and those who wanted to embrace change, which was increasingly being influenced by the working classes.

In fact, it could be argued that there was a strong link between sport and patriotism and that sometimes it was difficult, especially in the second half of the nineteenth century, to separate the links between the sports field and actual conflict. It was as though the involvement in sports and recreation was preparing people for a much wider life in society. Life in nineteenth century English public schools was often characterised by an obsession with sport, fighting, and brutal punishments, rather than with good working habits or a love of scholarship, and many Oxford University students commonly left the institution without a degree (Pugh, 1994, p. 67).

It was in the public schools in Britain where education, sports and discipline were deliberately interwoven, in order to create the next generation of British leaders. In fact, Jeffrey Richards, in the introduction to a book by Mangan (2000), was even stronger in his assessment of the importance of public schools to the development and enhancement of British values, and argued that they were an integral part of the nineteenth century revival of chivalry (Richards, 2000). Although initially resisted and disliked as a game not fit for gentlemen, by the second half of the nineteenth century, football was considered a gentleman's game associated with public schools. According to Mangan, during the second half of the nineteenth century for example, the playing of games, and in particular, attendance at football was compulsory (Mangan, 2000, p. 75). Prestigious British schools such Harrow was not alone in this regard, as the playing of football was not only played in most of the public schools in the country. It was not surprising then, that Andrew Watson should have excelled in so many different sports like high jump, rowing, rugby and football, as the quality of schools he attended, would have concentrated on such games. The schools where he was a pupil, were imbued with such middle class social values, and would have regarded sports as critical components of their curriculum.

It was partly as a result of the influence of the middle classes in the second half of the nineteenth century, that the English Football Association in 1863 was established (Pugh, 1994). However, from then on, it was the popular agitations and practices of the working classes which influenced the further developments in the game. Nowhere was this conflict of interest more apparent, than in the debate between amateurism and professionalism, or perhaps more aptly, between those who wished to preserve the existing kind of game for the elites primarily in the south of England, and those who wished to see radical changes which would have more of a greater appeal to the working classes. In essence, therefore, the clash between the supporters of professionalism and the proponents of amateur sports was also a clash between the social elites from the south and the urban working class from the industrialised north of the country.

These Victorian attitudes pertaining to sports and leisure were also accompanied by varying degrees of snobbery and superiority. According to Lorimer (1996), it was widely assumed in some circles that it was the British aristocracy who should be responsible for being agents of Western civilisation in order to transform other peoples' lives (Lorimer, 1996, p. 23). This is why, at the beginning of the nineteenth century in Britain, under the banner of laissez-faire capitalism, slavery could be abolished, on the grounds of its inhumanity, whereas the late nineteenth century colonial advocates of economic and political domination of Africa, had very little hesitation in perpetuating the idea of separate and unequal development, if this helped in exploiting raw materials for processing in Europe. Robinson and Gallagher (1985) began their discussion by pointing out how the Victorians regarded themselves as leaders of civilisation and also pioneers of industry and progress. The Victorian outlook was based on the view that they had been imbued with a strong sense of superiority and self-righteousness. These qualities were taught or emphasised in the main public schools, which were located primarily in the south of the country.

Thomas Arnold, who was headmaster at Rugby School between 1828 and 1848, believed that one way of attempting to gain control over the sons of the elite within their schools was to develop some kind of sporting agenda. Furthermore, the Victorians were convinced of the relationship between the physical, mental, and moral health. The Victorian public school thus became a beacon of institutions filled with the responsibility of helping to create this new British breed of young men who were imbued with the two key social features of a strong physical and moral bearing. It was this development of the muscular Christianity in young men, which was seen as a necessary component in the up-bringing of every public-educated school boy. The new ruling class during the Victorian period believed that the playing of team sports would contribute to this purpose, as it was felt that games helped to shape character. According to Goldblatt (2007), sport therefore played an important role in hardened up the Victorian ruling class, for the task of imperial conquest and global hegemony (Goldblatt, 2007, pp. 26, 27).

That the level of interest in sports had reached the very elite within Britain can be seen with regard to the way certain sports activities were taken seriously by government officials. In the House of Commons on 25 May 1875, the Member of Parliament, Mr Gathorne Hardy, proposed that the Parliament adjourn so that members of the House could, if they wanted, go to the Derby horse-racing event. This motion was vehemently opposed by Sir Wilfrid Lawson. What is even more interesting was the fact that this report also pointed out that such a motion had previously been raised in the year 1847. The argument was, that the late Prime Minister had, in 1872, argued that horse-racing was a noble, manly and distinguished national sport' (Hansard Parliamentary Debates, 25 May 1875).

The nature of the football played in the 1870s in Britain was dominated by people from the upper class. The FA Cup finals in the first few years of its existence featured the Edwards brothers who were both former students at Eton. Furthermore, one of the brothers, Alfred Edwards, not only played cricket for England, but later served as an MP and a member of the British Cabinet. Such was the dominance and influence of the social elite class in football in Britain at this time, that in 1873, the FA Cup final was delayed so that the crowd and the players could get to the football game but also get an opportunity to attend

Varsity Boat Race which had also been scheduled for that day (Glodblatt, 2007, p. 33). In addition, in some sports such as horse-racing and rowing, these were financially backed by members of the aristocracy. This was done largely through means of gambling which was prevalent among the very rich and powerful in England from as early as the eighteenth century. In this way, they became the backers of a number of sporting events especially boxing, rowing and horse-racing (Goldblatt, 2007, pp. 21, 22).

Muscular Christians took team sports to the urban working class in an effort to evangelise through sports (Vamplew, 1988, p. 12). The sport of football was regarded by many from within the social elite, as 'manly and fit for English men as it puts courage into their hearts to meet an enemy in the face' (Lowerson, 1995, p. 82). Religion was also linked to sports, in that many Sunday schools were seen as nurseries to extend adult church attendance. For this reason religious clubs and associations increasingly offered sports, especially football and cricket as key attractions. Queen's Park Football Club grew out of the YMCA and Hibernian formed in 1875, was established out of the Catholic Young Men's Society (Huggins, 2004, p. 41). It was precisely to ensure that these moral and ethical values were firmly instilled in their team, which formed a significant part of the mission of Britain's most elitist amateur football club, the Corinthians, for whom Andrew Watson would prove to be a critical player.

Amateurism, Elitism and Corinthians Football Club

Andrew Watson played for two of the greatest amateur football clubs in Britain. We have examined his involvement with the Queen's Park Club. The other club was Corinthians of London. Part of the reason for the establishment of the Corinthians Club was as a reaction against the dominance of the Scottish over the English in football matches. As we have seen, the Scottish national team was so strong during the 1870s and 1880s that, of the first fifteen games played between the national teams of England and Scotland from 1872 to the end of the 1880s, only once did England beat Scotland (Vasili, 1998, p. 60).

It was this constant general pattern of Scottish triumphs over England, which concerned the English Football Association and its then honorary assistant secretary, N.L. Jackson in 1882. In particular, the Football Association were anxious to discover the reasons for the weaknesses in the teams representing England. According to Cavallini, Jackson's special foresight was his recognition that while the Scottish players had frequent opportunities of playing together, very few of the English players even had the opportunity to meet on the same ground except in international matches (Cavillini, 2007, p. 7). It was in this context, that the Corinthians Football Club was established in 1882. Jackson's dream of establishing a team which could challenge the Scottish dominance over England was partially achieved. From the middle of the 1880s through to the 1890s, the England national football teams were able to mount far more effective resistance against the Scots, helped in part, by the inclusion of players from the Corinthians Football Club (Cavillini, 2007, p. 7).

To say that Jackson was a keen sports enthusiast would probably be an understatement. Not only was he a significant member of the English Football Association, he had founded the Finchley Football Club in 1874 and was also a founding member of the Lawn Tennis Association. In addition, N.L. Jackson was a journalist who wrote about amateur sports, particularly those played by the social elites such as lawn tennis and golf (Birley, 1995, p. 33). According to Gibbons, 'Pa Jackson's' Corinthians idea was based on the belief that England's regular defeats at the hands of the Scots were due to a lack of understanding among the players, rather than a general deficiency of skill. Therefore, the Corinthians Football Club was to be established based only on the use of the finest players in England gathered together to 'develop a team spirit equal to that of the Scots (Gibbons, 2001, p. 66). That this was, from its inception, an exclusive club, can be seen from the fact that there was to be a membership, limited to only fifty carefully selected people. This is why the claim is made in this study, that Andrew Watson's very inclusion in this team was clearly indicative of his overall ability as a player, as well as his social standing in the community.

Cavallini suggests that there are at least two possible reasons for the selection of the name Corinthians. First, it is believed that the name was possibly chosen by the men gathered at the second meeting of the football club in 1882 because of the wealth and affluence and prominence of the Ancient Greek city of Corinth. This ancient city was not only believed to rival Athens, but also boasted of the slogan '*Ou pantos plein es Korinthon*' which, when translated means, 'not everyone is able to go to Corinth' due then, to the high cost of living there. By extension, this meant, as far as the Corinthians Football Club was concerned, that not anyone could play for them. However, Cavillini points out that the more accurate reason for the choosing of the name, was due to the original meaning of the word, 'man of fashion and pleasure' (Cavallini, 2007, p. 9). This, he felt, best encapsulated the very essence and mission of the team.

That Corinthians Football Club was an elitist club can be seen, not only through its name and overall mission to raise the level or standard of the English game, but also in its very selective and socially exclusive membership. Although there was no official written code to the effect, it was accepted as an unwritten code, that only players from public schools or those who had attended university who were very good at football, should be selected to join the club. In other words, only members of the British social elite could play for this club. It is in this sense, therefore, that Andrew Watson's inclusion in this elite team was only possible, because he was considered, by Corinthians at least, as a member of the socially elite in Britain. The mission of the football club is perhaps captured by the quote below;

> When one is at school, there is the feeling that the sense of pride … can never be surpassed; when the schoolboy goes to the varsity, he finds that love of his school is swallowed up in an altogether stronger feeling – a sentiment almost reverence – towards his university. It is a feeling which nerves him to do all things for the honour of the alma mater… this feeling is carried on to the Corinthian FC. They know that they have the honour to be members of a club without rival, and their desire is to help retain that position (Cavallini, 2007, p. 62).

To be a member of this exclusive gentleman's club, meant individuals had to belong to the social elite of British society. Wealth, education, good leadership skills, fairness and team spirit, as well as a commitment to amateurism, were all considered crucial elements of this team's ethos and ambition.

The First game played by the Corinthians was on 26 October 1882 against St Thomas's Hospital, based on the adoption of a 2-2-6 formation in which Corinthians won 2-1 (Cavallini, 2007, p. 10). As we have seen, this was in fact, a new pioneering formation, based on the Scottish model, rather than the previously established 1-1-8 formation, with its emphasis individualism and dribbling skills. On 18 January 1883 Corinthians played Upton Park and were solidly thrashed 7-0. It was, however, in this game that the secretary of Queen's Park Club and Scottish international, Andrew Watson made his debut for the Corinthians Club, thus becoming the first Black player to play for this elite football team. This was not the best of starts for Watson, but thereafter, things improved significantly. A few months later, in a game against Church Football Club on 24 March 1883, in which Corinthians won 2-0, two defenders, Andrew Watson and Holme as well as the goal-keeping exploits of Swepstone, were singled out for special mention as their performance helped Corinthians from conceding any goals (Cavallini, 2007, p. 12). Their victory over Blackburn Rovers on their own ground by 8-1 in 1884 was truly remarkable and also marked a turning point, in that this signalled the start of Corinthians' dominance in British football for the next two decades. In the heart of the defence of the Corinthians team in 1883 and 1884 was Andrew Watson. In this resounding victory for the Corinthians, when they beat Blackburn Rover 8-1, Andrew Watson was actually playing right back for them (Robinson, 1920, p. 144). In the 1884 season also, Corinthians beat Preston North End who were regarded as one of the very best teams in the country at that time.

According to Taylor, the Corinthians Club was the 'pride of the gentlemen amateur game … or an amateur super-club' (Taylor, 2008, p. 83). Jackson's philosophy of selecting only the very best amateur players paid rich dividend. By the 1885-1886 football season nine of their team represented England and when England beat Wales in 1894, the entire eleven players were from the Corinthians Club. Although Taylor describes them as one of the best teams in the country during the last decade of the nineteenth century, when it is taken into account that they were able to provide the entire England team in 1894 and 1895 against Wales as well as beating FA Cup holders Bury 10-3 in 1904 (Taylor, 2008, p. 83), it is difficult to regard them as anything other, than the very best team at this period in British football history. The season of 1884 was when the club really came to national prominence when they beat Blackburn Rovers 8-1. Blackburn Rovers had recently beaten Queen's Park. They played with five forwards who would make long passes into spaces for other players to run into (Mason, 1974, p. 216). It is interesting to note that two of the members of the Corinthians team in this match had been selected from Queens Park, Dr John Smith who actually captained the Corinthians team, and the other former Queen's Park player was Watson (Robinson, 1920, p. 145).

During the nine years prior to the 1884-1885 football season, England had only one victory against Scotland. During the next nine years there were forty four Corinthians players who played in the various English teams. During this period four games were won by England over Scotland and three were drawn and two were lost. This, according to Robinson, was indicative of N.L Jackson's view, that combination and playing together were vital factors on the road to success in football (Robinson, 1920, p. 146). Jackson's aim was to give good players more frequent opportunities of playing together as the want of combination based on passing as well as dribbling, was strikingly apparent in the English international team as compared with those representing Scotland (Robinson, 1920, p. 145).

The main purpose of Corinthians was to showcase the very best amateur footballers in Britain. In 1886 the England team which drew 1-1 with Scotland, included two players from Blackburn Rovers and nine from Corinthians. In effect, Corinthians had followed the tradition of looking north of the border in order to find the very best talent. Watson would have been eligible to play for this top English amateur side only because of his public school and university education as well as his remarkable football ability as an amateur player.

From the beginning, two features made the Corinthians Club stand out from most others at the time. First, the club selected players only from public or university educated backgrounds and secondly, they insisted on selecting players who were non-professionals, thus ensuring the club's amateur status. The main principle of the Corinthian team was that gentlemanly conduct would always be observed and, where an infringement occurred, this, it was assumed, should be regarded as an accident and so it would be improper to take unfair advantage of an opponent (Goldblatt, 2007, p. 48). Such was their focus on fair play that it was reported that in one game in the 1930s when the match referee failed to turn up, the captain of the Corinthians team stepped in to referee the game while also playing, and actually awarded a free kick against himself (Russell, 1997, p. 92).

For the amateur players, certain key features of sportsmen were crucial such as teamwork and discipline, obedience to leaders, order and hard work. For Holt, one of the most important elements was the issue of 'fair play which was considered to be the watchword of the gentleman amateur' (Holt, 1989, p. 98). This meant, not only playing by the rules, but more important, by the spirit of the game. A true amateur would not seek to gain any advantage over an opponent. This goes a far way to explain why the Corinthians Football Club, as will be discussed shortly, would withdraw their goal-keeper if a penalty was awarded against them, on the principle that it would be wrong not to accept the principle of a foul, even if it had been an accident (Holt, 1989, p. 99). In an ideal situation, it was not considered appropriate or befitting of someone from the very social elite, to engage in activities which demanded them to 'toil and sweat for their laurels.' Furthermore, too much practising was seen to undermine natural grace and talent (Holt, 1989, p. 100), although the team did spend some time in practice together.

This can further be seen with regard to Jackson's support and almost insistence that where professionals and amateurs played on the same England team, it was the preserve of the amateur to always be chosen as captain. This was a last ditched attempt by those like Jackson, representing the old order who wished to ensure a continuation of the existing elite social class structure in sport. For example, in 1891 when England played Scotland in football, the one amateur player available for England had to be the captain. Speaking more generally on this issue of captaincy, Jackson was reported to have said, 'paid football players are supposed to be inferior in manners and breeding' (Birley, 1995, p. 36).

Despite this elitist composition and its Victorian and Christian ethos within the organisation, the quality of the football remained very high, and wherever the Corinthians team went to play, they received considerable praise for their style of football and moral behaviour and conduct on the field of play. Cavallini summed it up by saying;

> The Corinthians style has been unique and never entirely absent, even in the club's worst years… the forwards play a good open game… taking the ball on the run and making straight for the goal without dallying. The passing is crisp, quick and along the ground; the shooting is done from all angles… there is never a suspicion of foul play. The impression one gleans from watching the Corinthians is that they play to win the game and to enjoy the game while doing so (Cavallini, 2007, p. 62).

An indication of their ethos towards the game can be seen from the fact that they were opposed to the penalty kick rule, which was introduced in 1891. According to Taylor, the very idea of penalising a team for a deliberate foul was an 'anathema to the notion of gentlemanly sporting behaviour,' thus resulting in the Corinthians deliberately kicking the ball wide if they were awarded a penalty kick and withdrawing their goal-keeper if they conceded a penalty (Taylor, 2008, p. 84). Blythe Smart was much more forceful on this issue by pointing out that the Corinthians were so peeved by the introduction of the penalty kick, that their goal-keeper would stand by the post when the spot kick was taken (Blythe Smart, 2003, p. 14). However,

Cavallini has pointed out that there were no records suggesting that the Corinthians goal-keeper actually did this during games or that their forwards would deliberately miss the spot kicks rather than score whenever they were awarded penalties (Cavallini, 2007). As far as Jackson was concerned, he considered it an 'insult to the honour of a gentleman, to suggest that he would either deliberately commit a foul or stoop to take advantage of an opponent's transgressions' (Birley, 1995, p. 36).

It was inevitable, however, that for all of Jackson's best efforts, the tide of power, influence and popular opinion was changing. According to Taylor, he represented a dying breed which hoped to keep the game within the elite social class and, thereby, encourage the playing of football for sporting reasons rather than professionally for money (Taylor, 2008). By the late nineteenth century, there was a growing concern over the nature of the football game based on the league competition and the FA Cup, which had helped to debase the game (Birley, 1995, p. 34). Birley makes reference to the fact that by the 1890s there were signs of popular adulations being given to individual footballers in the form of street ovations, photographs in shop widows, glowing newspaper articles, as well an overall increase in the level of gambling associated with the game (Birley, 1995, p. 34).

Despite these changes, the Corinthians remained firmly committed to their amateur status and such was their quality and high standard, they, like Queen's Park in Scotland, were able to seriously challenge the top professional clubs in England until the early part of the twentieth century. An indication of this can be seen with reference to the 1904 season, when the Corinthians beat the English FA Cup champions, Bury 10-3 (Walvin, 1994b, p. 92). Bury had earlier won the cup final by a resounding 6-0. The fact that Corinthians could beat them by 10-3 shows their strength and dominance during this period although they were only committed to playing friendly matches because they refused to join the professional league.

Corinthians was also the first English team to play a football match outside Europe and, in particular, in 1897 became the first foreign team to visit South Africa. By 1914 they had embarked on fourteen overseas tours, including two further trips to South Africa (Raath, 2002, p. 4). In the first tour of South Africa, the English team returned home undefeated, but by 1907 the Corinthians only managed to win half of their twenty four games and were beaten on five occasions. This clearly demonstrates that the quality and standard of football being played in South Africa was improving (Raath, 2002, p. 4). Furthermore, it should be borne in mind that of the one hundred and fifty two tour matches the Corinthians played overseas, in countries like Brazil, Canada and the United Sates, they lost only eleven games and six of those were to the South Africans (Raath, 2002, p. 4). This is further testimony to the overall contribution and development this one club gave to the spread and subsequent globalisation of football. Despite their good standard of football, their social class elitist backgrounds and attitudes were present. For example, this might be one of the reasons why they made disparaging remarks about the dirtiness and verbosity of the natives in the Madeira Islands on their way to one of their tours of South Africa (Cavallini, 2007, p. 48).

Between 5 August and 24 September 1910 the Corinthians went on a tour to Brazil. The team played a number of games and such was their brilliant style and overall performances, that in Sao Paulo, a group of Sao Paulo Railway men decided to form a team and it was called Corinthians. Thus the Corinthians Paulista Football Club of Sao Paulo Brazil was formed in 1910. This club went on to become one of the greatest teams in Brazil winning one FIFA World Club Championship as well as four Brazilian Championships (Cavallini, 2007, pp. 107, 108). Perhaps it should come as no surprise that the influence and legacy of the Corinthians of London seemed to have had a lasting legacy on the Brazilian style of play even in recent times. Indeed Cavallini pointed out that the pre-war National Amateur Cups champions of Real Madrid, Corinthians Paulista and the Hungarian and Swedish teams were all influenced by the Corinthians FC (Cavallini, 2007, p. 227). In this way it can be seen that the Corinthians went on to shape and influence the very nature of how the game of football was played in Brazil, Hungary and Spain.

But how was it that this amateur club was so outstanding for the better part of fifty years? Cavallini suggests that there were at least two important factors which might help to explain this. Firstly, their players had been playing the game from they were boys and therefore enjoyed organised football long before the majority of the professionals of that era. In addition, they were better fed, better housed and protected by better medical advice (Cavallini, 2007, p. 62).

One of the reasons for the decline of the Corinthians team came about because of the lack of the regular quality opposition of amateur teams especially in the twentieth century. After 1907 more and more of the better quality clubs in England became part of the English Association and were part of the professional game. To make matters worse, the English Association forbade their members from playing against teams which were not part of the same association. In this way the Corinthians became increasingly isolated and weaker through lack of regular quality opposition to play against (Cavallinin, 2007, p. 94). They remained an amateur club until they were disbanded in 1939.

During the very early formative years in the 1880s when the ethos, philosophy and standards of play of Corinthians were being established, Andrew Watson was selected to be part of this team. Because Watson had been educated at one of the very best secondary schools in London and had gone on to enrol at university, he was eligible to be considered for selection at Corinthians. An additional factor was of course, because of the amount of money left for him after the death of his father. The Corinthians was Britain's most elite and exclusive gentlemen's amateur football club and had a membership of about fifty people and so for Watson to be invited to join them shows he was an extraordinary player and personality. The Corinthians Football Club was a socially elitist football club, which, for a time, was Britain's, and arguably, the world's best club team. From its very inception, only the very best of British talent could be selected for membership. For Watson to have been selected to play in such a team speaks volumes about his character, social standing and ability.

Conclusion

This chapter has shown that a very significant factor in the early development of football in Britain was the influence of the socially elite and powerful. However, as the nineteenth century drew to a close, the emergent clashes between those wishing to preserve amateurism in football and the supporters of popular change and professionalism, became increasingly polarised. The establishment of the Corinthians football Club was essentially an attempt to preserve the traditional values of Victorian Britain. Their style of passing the ball with great speed and accuracy as well as their insistence on fair play with a strong desire to win was a major hallmark of that tradition. Within a year of their establishment in 1882, drawing on only the very best players available, the club was able to call upon the services of Andrew Watson. Therefore if we accept that the Corinthians Football Club was at the cutting edge of pioneering the development of football in Britain and the world, then Andrew Watson would certainly qualify as the world's first Black football pioneer.

CHAPTER SEVEN

Andrew Watson the Legend and His Legacy

This chapter attempts to pull together three key points about Andrew Watson's story and considers why he should be remembered and honoured, both in Britain as well as in Guyana where he was born. The first of these three points centres on his social standing in elite British society. Secondly, the chapter assesses his achievements in the game as a player, administrator and investor in football. The third area of concentration focuses on the fact of Andrew Watson's unfortunate inadequate recognition in the country of his birth, where he is virtually like an unknown soldier.

To be a member of the social elite of nineteenth century Britain, one had to have either land or property rights, or wealth through industrial trades or commerce. Another way was, of course, to be bequeathed a generous amount of wealth through inheritance. It was in this sense that Watson (and his sister Annette) acquired the initial means of financial success. In addition, it must be borne in mind that Andrew Watson's father was a plantation owner whose family had long connections with property in Demerara for at least two generations (David Alston *www.slavesandhighlanders*). In addition, Watson had the privilege of attending two of the country's finest public schools as well as later enrolling for university education at Glasgow University.

Notwithstanding his ethnicity or Blackness, Andrew Watson was a highly respected member of the social elite within British society during the late nineteenth century. This is important because at the time he lived and played football in Britain, a person's social background was a critical factor in helping to determine a person's overall development, personality, employment prospects and the nature of the very people they associated with. Watson also played for two of the greatest amateur teams in Britain, Queen's Park and then Corinthians

One of the marks of a true gentleman during the Victorian period was that they should engage in sports for the love and joy of it, rather than for the sake of money. Throughout Watson's football career, he seemed to have remained loyal to this commitment of being an amateur player, though embryonic professionalism, through informal means, was also taking place in the mid 1880s when he was playing.

It was a combination of these qualities which made it possible for Watson to become a member of the Corinthians Football Club. It was taken for granted that these players were men of means, as well as recipients of the best education which Victorian Britain could provide. Therefore, there should have been no need for them to resort to sports as a means of income. The members of the Corinthians team were, by virtue of being selected, established members of the social elite of Britain. Amateurism was a feature of the aristocratic life style of Britain. And, as Thomas puts it, in his description of eighteenth and nineteenth century British culture, the two outstanding features of society were, that it was 'overwhelmingly aristocratic and also cosmopolitan' (Thomas, 1985, p. 282).

Part of the objective of the Corinthians Football club was to internationalise football, and to help spread key aspects of the Victorian and British culture such as loyalty, where people would go the extra mile to play for their team and achieve success through hard work and fairness. It was thought that these could be achieved through sportsmanship and a sense of belonging to a very special organisation. During Victorian times, leisure and recreation were often associated with the family. The family was the cardinal sign of respectability and recreation. Family meals, the ritual of tea, family strolls in the park, visiting relatives on Sundays, and family holidays all reinforced the significance of this core aspect of Victorian life (Black, 1973, p. 252). The fact that Watson played for the Corinthians Club, also demonstrated that he must have been considered by adherents and fellow associates of the British elite (in football at least), to be perfectly eligible for such exclusive membership.

It is truly remarkable that Watson was regarded not only as a good footballer, but also part of Britain's elite. He managed to achieve this, because of his overall accomplishments in football, his upbringing and education and also his personal wealth. Although there does not appear to be much evidence of any degree of racist abuse or discrimination towards Andrew Watson personally on the field or otherwise, we are aware, for example, that his very team mate at Parkgrove Football Club, Robert Walker, was the subject of racial abuse while probably playing in the same matches as Watson. It would seem surprising for these kinds of racist abuse to have singled out one Black player and not the other. Furthermore, If Watson received no such racist verbal abuse; one has to wonder why he was not singled out, while his team mate was. Was it because he was a better player, or, notwithstanding his Blackness or ethnicity, was it because of his high social standing within Glasgow? Nor can it be claimed that such racist abuse disappeared soon after the second half of the 1870s when Watson and Walker played together. As we have already seen earlier in this study, Arthur Wharton, who played in the late 1880s and 1890s, and Walter Tull who played in the early years of the twentieth century, both experienced varying degrees of racial discrimination and verbal abuse. Vasili, for example, makes the point that racism was present among the hierarchy who governed English football during the 1880s, and this was a critical factor which made it difficult for Black players, such as Arthur Wharton to have been selected for the England national team (Vasili, 1998, p.77).

Without the primary or other forms of concrete evidence to answer these questions, it is difficult to be conclusive as to whether Watson denied or played-down his ethnicity or Blackness, or simply concentrated on his performances on the field. What is very evident, however, was that Watson seemed to 'rise above any prejudice against his colour' and attained some remarkable achievements (Mitchell, 2013). Nor should it be assumed that it was impossible for some Black people in Britain to gain widespread acceptability during the eighteenth and nineteenth centuries, similar to that achieved by Andrew Watson. There is no doubt that discrimination was rife in Britain and there was a generally held perception among many White British people that the role of Black people was to be i‧

positions of servitude. Little informs us that it became fairly common in England from the seventeenth century at least for little Black boys to work as servants especially by some White elites who dressed them up as exotically as possible, where they were often treated as pets (Little, 1972, p. 189). In fact, he claims that so popular was it to see Black people in positions of servitude, that in Garrick's portrayal of Othello as a Black person, it was believed to have provoked the ironic comments of why was he not presented as someone bringing in the tea-kettle and lamp (Little, 1972, p. 189).

Despite the social hardships and discrimination faced by many Black people in Britain during the colonial era, there were a small number of them who, unlike the majority of Black people at the time, lived in relative comfort, wealth and enjoyed a veneer at least, of some social opportunity. Eighteenth century writers such as Ignatius Sancho and Oluadah Equiano, or Francis Barber, a former Jamaican slave, who ran a school near Lichfield, are examples of Black people who gained some degree of popularity, respectability and even possible acceptability within the White affluent circles. Shyllon, for example, made reference to the sword-fencing Black man called Soubsie, who was in the care of the Duchess of Queensberry or the amazing accomplishments of 'Mr George' a Black man who lived in Paris in the late eighteenth century and was not only a fine swordsman, but was also someone who spoke many different languages and was apparently bright and articulate (Shyllon, 1977, pp. 42, 43). Some Black people acquired wealth and patronage and were received 'without reservation in the very highest circles' of British society. The Chevalier Georges de St. George, son of the Marquis de Langey, was a personal friend of the Prince of Wales, who would later become George 1V (Little, 1972, p. 221). In this sense, therefore, Andrew Watson should also be considered as one of a small group of Black people in Britain, whose outstanding achievements received some degree of national respect and acknowledgement.

The second point which has to be noted with regard to the Watson story, was not only his overall achievements as an outstanding footballer, but also his roles with two different football clubs as club administrator or secretary as well as financial investor in the development of football in the Govan area of Glasgow. In addition, by travelling to play football in England, he was, therefore, Britain's first 'Black Scottish professor' who made a significant contribution in helping to spread the development of the modern game of football to parts of England. The fact that Watson played for the very best teams at the highest levels possible, and helped them to defeat their closest rivals, means that both domestically and internationally, this was equivalent to a modern player winning the domestic league competition and the FIFA World Cup. No other British club teams were as powerful as the Queen's Park team and the Corinthians. In similar fashion, the Scottish national football team was, during much of the 1870s and 1880s, the very best national team in the world. Watson was privileged to play for these three teams. He, of course, not only played for them, but, from most of the patchy accounts available, generally performed well. For a Black man to have been selected for the best team in the word during this period in British history was truly amazing. But for a Black man to have been appointed as of a national team at this period was even more remarkable.

In addition to his football abilities and achievements, Watson was also involved in football administration. The role of the club secretary in the 1870s and 1880s was a very important job in football. This role required the secretary to organise matches, deal with correspondences and some team affairs, although not necessarily always to deal with matters with regard to team selection and training. Although this job was often done on a voluntary basis during the period when Watson played, it was an important job. This demonstrated another aspect of Watson character, which was his leadership quality. This was another important feature of the kind of training he would have received from the quality of the secondary schools he attended. That he was able to carry out this role at the Parkgrove and Queen's Park clubs was clear evidence of his all-round abilities and the level of respect he must have had at the time.

We saw a sense of his leadership quality when he was invite to chair the meeting in the late 1870s regarding the propos

Scottish tour of Canada which never materialised. Watson had been invited to chair this meeting and, also made an invaluable suggestion and solid advice about the feasibility of the trip, which demonstrated excellent business acumen and overall professional judgement. It seemed that his decision and advice were generally well received and acted upon, which is indicative of the significance with which the other members must have taken his suggestion. Considering that Watson was, at this time, in his early twenties, this in itself was very remarkable.

An area to which we have not been able to provide much evidence in this study, is that of his possible financial contribution to the development of a ground for the Parkgrove Football team in the 1870s. We are not clear to what extent he might have also been involved, but it seems reasonably clear, as indicated in chapter three of this study, that he may have given some financial backing to the club which helped them to possibly find a suitable ground on which to play. It seems that Watson used some of his personal finance to invest in the football and, with his managerial involvement in Parkgrove, meant he was personally involved in the finances, administration and as well as being a member of the team in the 1870s.

We have seen, in chapter two that the former Black boxer Tom Molineaux fought for the title of British heavy weight boxing champion in 1810, but was unfairly beaten by a White English boxer named Tom Cribb. Molineaux's trainer and promoter was also a Black man named Bill Richmond, who had himself, been beaten by Tom Cribb in 1805. Richmond was a former slave in America but had come to Britain in the late eighteenth century in an attempt to make his fortune in boxing but never quite made it. Both these very good Black sportsmen were unable to fully realise their sporting ambitions or dreams. Much of this was due to the racist discriminatory practices which militated against them. It was, therefore, a very rare occurrence to find a Black person, like Andrew Watson, who in nineteenth century Britain, had managed to achieve such high level of influence and prestige within his sport and also the local community in Glasgow.

The third point which needs to be made with regard to the Watson story, centres on why he deserves to be remembered and celebrated in Guyana and Britain. Cristiano Ronaldo plays for Real Madrid, which is regarded as one of the best club teams in world football, as well as Portugal which is one of the top national teams in the world. Lionell Messi plays for another top team in the form of Barcelona as well as for Argentina which is regarded higher up the FIFA rankings than Portugal. Pele played for the top Brazilian team as well as Brazil itself when it was arguably the best team in the world. These three names, as well as Diego Maradona of Argentina, are regarded by many, as the best players ever to grace football fields. If we consider that Andrew Watson played for the two very best club teams in the world, also captained his national team when they were regarded as the very best team in the world. It seems strange that this Caribbean-born footballer is never considered as a sporting great and football pioneer. If we were to create a list of the world's greatest ever footballers who contributed the most to the playing and development of the sport, it would be a travesty not to include Watson's name. As we have seen, he was more than just a great player. For his life and dedication to the development of football, he deserves to be remembered and commemorated on a far grander scale than has hitherto been the case.

Watson only spent a few years in Guyana where he was born, before being sent by his father to live in Britain, but had considerable family roots in the country. At least three generations of the Watson family lived in Guyana. Notwithstanding the fact that Watson's family were part of the British White social elite who, by virtue of their social status, position and wealth, exploited the local Black population, he could legitimately claim to have strong family connections with Guyana. Just as we saw in the first two chapters of this book, both his name and general memory seems to have been forgotten within the context of Guyanese history, and also what could be called Guyanese Diasporic History. Watson's name is not included as one of Guyana's national heroes since he was not involved in campaigning for the Guyanese country or its peoples. Quite rightfully, some of the names of Guyana's national hero include Kofi from Ghana who led a rebellion in 1763 in Berbice. It also includes Quamina the slave, also from Ghana, who was instrumental in the Demerara Rebellion of 1823. In the twentieth century, other notable figures such as former President Forbes Burnham and President Hoyte, as well as national poet Martin Carter, have all been inducted into the country's hall of fame.

Very few Guyanese people today would strongly disagree with these names being included in the list. However, this study asks, whether Watson's name could at least be remembered and honoured in some way, despite the fact that his footballing career and achievements were done for Scottish and English football teams, rather than any of the Guyanese football teams which were emerging in the late 1880s and early 1890s. It was not until 1880 that the Georgetown Football Club was formed. By the latter part of the nineteenth century, the boys at this Guyanese elite school had started promoting development of the sport of football. Had Watson's father been inclined, he might have sent his son to Queen's College, Guyana which had been established in 1844, and perhaps Andrew Watson might have become a keen sports person there and develop his football interests and skills. This, however, is conjecture and never happened, as he was sent to Britain instead. This year marks one hundred years since the Battle of the Somme during World War 1. Many British footballers were killed in this, and other battles, during the war. One of these was Walter Tull who was killed in 1918 in France. Efforts are currently underway to commemorate Tull's life and achievements. Similarly, a few days ago a statue was unveiled in London to mark the outstanding achievements and sacrifices of the Jamaican-born nurse Mary Seacole. She was particularly significant for her efforts during the war in the Crimea in the 1850s.

It would be entirely appropriate, though, as Guyana looks to its fiftieth year of political independence, to consider having Watson's profile raised. If a special commemoration could recently be done to Watson's memory in London, and he has also been recently inducted into the Scottish Football Museum's hall of fame in 2012, it seems both ironic and tragic that he is not mentioned, acknowledged or better appreciated in Guyana. Perhaps, if nothing else, this book serves as a reminder to the Guyanese people of his contributions to the development of the modern game and therefore, calls for his name to be much more visibly recognised and acknowledged in the country of his birth.

Conclusion

What this study has shown is that Andrew Watson was a remarkable footballer who played at the very highest level for club and country. Whilst many studies on the history of football in Britain have not mentioned or acknowledge his presence or contributions, he was part of the wave of Scottish 'professors' who came south of the border to play for English teams and help to develop the combination style of football based on dribbling as well as passing. Even though he played as an amateur, Watson's achievements as a footballer, could certainly rival, if not surpass those of Arthur Wharton and Walter Tull. He played for the best national team at the time and also played for the two best amateur clubs in Britain. Andrew Watson was unique in that he was able to bring together a number of crucial personal qualities and features which enabled him to achieve a degree of social acceptability and respect among his White football peers. These in turned ensured that he was able to play the game at the very highest level possible for an amateur player at that time. Watson was educated, wealthy, a skilful and experienced football administrator and arguably, one of Britain's best footballers. Despite the fact that Watson played during the period when the amateur game was still the dominant form, for a Black footballer originally from the Guyana to have played in the very top teams in the world and be part of the Scottish influence which changed the nature of football in England, and ultimately the rest of the world, is truly unbelievable and helps to support the main being made in this book, that he was certainly the world's first Black football superstar.

REFERENCES

Alston, David (2014) *'The Habits of These Creatures in Clinging One to the Other, Enslaved Africans, Scots and the Plantations of Guyana*, unpublished paper

Alston, David www.spanglefish.com/slavesandhighlanders/index.asp?pageid=299951 accessed 13 October 2014

Alston, David, (2014a) *A Forgotten Diaspora: the children of enslaved and free coloured women and Highland Scots in Guyana before Emancipation*, unpublished paper

Andrews, David and Jackson Steven eds. (2001) *Sport Stars: The cultural Politics of Sporting Celebrity*, London and New York, Routledge

Bains, Jas and Bowler, Dave (2001) *Samba in the Smethwick End: Regis, Cunningham, Batson and the Football Revolution*, Edinburgh and London, Mainstream Publishing Company

Beck, Peter (1999) *Scoring for Britain: International Football and International Politics, 1900-1939*, London, Frank Cass

Birley Derek (1995) *Land and Sport and Glory, Sport and British Society 1887-1910*, Manchester University Press

Birley, Derek (1988) Bonaparte and the Squire: Chauvinism, Virility and Sport in the Period of the French Wars in Mangan, J.A. eds. *Pleasure, Profit and Proselytism, British Culture and Sport at Home and Abroad 1700-1914*, London, Frank Cass

Black, Eugene eds. (1973) *Victorian Culture and Society*, New York, Evanston, San Francisco, London   Harper and Row Publishers

Blythe Smart, John (2003) *The WOW Factor: A Concise History of Early Soccer and the Men Who Made it*, London, Blythe Smart Publishers

Bone, D. D. (1890) *Scottish Football: Reminiscences and Sketches*, Glasgow, John Menzies Hay Nisbet and Company

Briggs, Asa (1968) *Victorian Cities*, London, Penguin Books

Cavallini, Rob (2007) *Play Up Corinth: A History of the Corinthian Football Club*, Stroud, Gloucestershire, Stadia, An Imprint of Tempus Publishers

Charles, Christopher eds. (2015) *Perspectives on Caribbean Football*, Hertfordshire, Hansib Publications Limited

Clark, Susan (2000) 'Up Against The Ropes, Peter Jackson as Uncle Tom in America, in *Drama Review, Vol. 14 No. 1*, New York University and Massachusetts Institute of Technology, pp. 157-182

Devine, T.M. (1990) *The Tobacco Lords: A Study of the Tobacco Merchants of Glasgow and Their Trading Activities*, Edinburgh University Press

Ferguson, James (2006) *World Class: An Illustrated History of Caribbean Football*, Oxford, MacMillan Caribbean Publishers

Fryer, Peter (1984) *Staying Power: The History of Black People in Britain*, London, Pluto Press

Galvin, Robert (2005) Football's Greatest Heroes, The National Football Museum Hall of Fame, London, Robson Book Publishers

Garland, Jon and Rowe, Michael (2001) *Racism and Anti-Racism in Football*, Hampshire, Palgrave Publishers

Gibbons, Philip (2001) *Association Football in Victorian England, A history of the from 1863 to 1900*, London, Minerva Press

Giulianotti, Richard and Robertson, Roland (2009) *Globalisation and Football*, London, SAGE Publications Ltd

Goldblatt, David (2007) *The Ball is Round: A Global History of Football*, London, Penguin Books

Golesworthy, Maurice (1972) *We Are The Champions: A History of the Football League Champions 1888-1972*, London, Pelham Books

Golesworthy, Maurice (1973) *The Encyclopaedia of Association Football*, London, Robert Hale Publishers

Hamilton, Al and Hinds, Rodney eds. (1999) *Black Pearls: The A-Z of Black Footballers in the English Game*, London, Hansib Publications

Hamilton, Douglas (2005) *Scotland, the Caribbean and the Atlantic World, 1750-1820*, Manchester University Press

Hansard Parliamentary Debates 9 April 1824 (http://hansard. millbanksystems.com/commons/1824/apr/09/building-of-new-churches) accessed 20 July 2015

Hansard Parliamentary Debates, 2 April, 1838 (http://hansard. millbanksystems.com/commons/1838/apr/02/the-hippodrome-nottinghill) accessed 4 August 2015

Hansard Parliamentary Debates, 25 May 1875, (http://hansard. millbanksystems.com/commons/1875/may/25/parliament-adjournment- accessed on 20 July 2015

Harvey, Adrian (2005) *Football: The First Hundred Years, The Untold Story*, London and New York, Routledge, Taylor and Francis Group

Heatley, Michael (2004) *A History of Football*, Gloucestershire, Green Umbrella Publishing

Hill, Tim (2008) *Encyclopaedia of World Football*, Bath, Parragon Publishers

Hinds, Rodney (2006) *Black Pearls: A History of Black Players in English Football*, Cheltenham, Sportsbooks Limited

Holt, Richard (1989) *Sport and the British, A Modern History*, Oxford University Press

Huggins, Mike (2004) *The Victorians and Sport*, London and New York, Hambledon and London Publishers

Hutchinson, John (1982) *The Football Industry*, Glasgow, Richard Drew Publishing Ltd,

Hutchinson, Roger (1996) *Empire Game: The British Invention of Twentieth Century Sport*, Edinburgh and London, Mainstream Publishing

Ismond, Patrick (2003) *Black and Asian Athletes in British Sport and Society, A Sporting Chance*, Hampshire, Palgrave Macmillan

Josiah, Barbara (2011) *Migration, Mining, and the African Diaspora: Guyana in the nineteenth and twentieth centuries,*, New York, Palgrave Macmillan,

Kyle, Donald (2015) *Sport and Spectacle in the Ancient World*, West Sussex, John Wiley and Sons Ltd,

Leafe, David (2010) 'The Shameful Story of How – 200 years ago this week – a bigoted Mob Cheated a Freed Slave out of the British Heavyweight Title', *The Mail Online* 14 December, http://www.dailymail.co.uk/news/article-1338673/200-years-ago-Black-Ajax-Thomas-Molineaux-cheated-British-heavyweight-title.html Accessed 21 January 2015

Little, Kenneth (1972) *Negroes in Britain: A Study of Race Relations in English Society*, London and Boston, Routledge and Kegan Paul

Lovesey, John (1993) Great Moments in British Sport: Legendary Triumphs and Dramas Relived, London, H.F. and G Witherby Publishers

Lorimer, Douglas (1996) 'Race, Science and Culture: Historical Continuities and Disccontinuities, 1850-1914, in West, Shearer eds. *The Victorians and Race*, Aldershot, Brookfield, USA, Ashgate Publishers

Lowerson, John (1995) *Sport and the English Middle Classes 1870-1914*, Manchester University Press

Lowndes, William (1952) *The Story of Football*, London, Thorsons Publishers

Mangan, J.A. (2000) *Athleticism in the Victorian and Edwardian Public School: The Emergence and Consolidation of an Educational Ideology*, London, Frank Cass Publishers

Martin, Tony (2012) *Caribbean History: From Pre-colonial Origins to the Present*, London, Pearson Publishers

Mason, Nicholas (1974) *The Story of all the World's Football Games*, London, Temple Smith

Mason, Tony (1980) Association Football and English Society 1863-1915, Sussex, Harvester Press Ltd

Mason, Tony eds. (1989) *Sport in Britain: A Social History*, Cambridge University Press

Mazrui, Ali (1986) *The Africans: A Triple Heritage*, London, BBC Publications

McBrearty, Richard, (2015) The Earliest Known Black Footballers, in show Racism the Red Card www.srtrc.org/news/news-and-events?news=5534 accessed 21 February 2016

Mclean, David (2014) 'Lost Edinburgh: The Football-Club' www.Scotsman.com/lifestyle/heritage/lost-edinburgh/the-football-club-1-3438950 10 June 2014, accessed 21 January 2015

Mitchell, Andy (2013) 'The Fate of Scotland's First Black Footballer Revealed' 20 March, www.scotsman.com/sport/football/latest/fa accessed on 17 June 2014

Moorhouse, H. (1984) 'Professional Football and Working Class Culture: English Theories and Scottish Evidence' *Sociological Review*, Vol. 32, pp. 285-315

Moore, Brian (1995) *Cultural Power Resistance and Pluralism: Colonial Guyana 1838-1900*, Kingston Jamaica, The Press University of the West Indies

Moore, Brian (1998) 'The Culture of the Colonial Elites of nineteenth-Century Guyana' in Johnson, Howards and Watson Karl eds. *The White Minority in the Caribbean*, Kingston, Oxford and Princeton, Ian Randle, James Curry and Markus Wiener Publishers

Murray, Bill (1984) *The Old Firm; Sectarianism, Sport and Society in Scotland*, Edinburgh, John Donald Publishers Ltd

Norridge, Julian (2008) Can *We Have Our Balls Back, Please: How the British Invented Sport*, London, Allen Lane, Penguin Group

Old International, (1896) *25 Years Football*, Glasgow and Edinburgh, John Menzies and Co.

Peterson, Bob (2011) *Peter Jackson: A Biography of the Australian Heavy Weight Champion, 1860-1901*, North Carolina, McFarland and Company Inc

Philip, Robert (2010) 'A Hero and a Football Pioneer, the National Sport, 8 March www.thenational.ae/sport/a-hero-and-a-football-pioneer accessed 13 October 2014

Pugh, Martin (1994) *State and Society, British Political and Social History 1870-1992*, London, New York, Edward Arnold

Raath, Peter (2002) *Soccer Through the Years 1862-2002: The first official history of South African Soccer*, The World Shop, (No publishing details) editor Michele Usher, www.soccerthroughtheages.com

Richards, Jeffrey (2000) in Mangan, J.A. *Athleticism in the Victorian and Edwardian Public School: The Emergence and Consolidation of an Educational Ideology*, London, Frank Cass Publishers

Robinson, Richard (1920) History of the Queen's Park Football Club 1867-1917, Glasgow, http://scottish-football-historical-archive.com/history accessed on 3 and 4th November 2014

Robinson, Ronald and Callagher, John with Denny, Alice, (1985) *Africa and the Victorians, the Official Mind of Imperialism*, London, MacMillan Publishers

Rose Michael (1985) 'the emergence of Urban Britain' in Haigh, Christopher eds. *The Cambridge Historical Encyclopedia of Great Britain and Ireland*, Cambridge University Press

Ruhomon, Peter (1988) *Centenary History of the East Indians in British Guiana 1838-1938*, Guyana, Published by the East Indians 150th Anniversary Committee,

Russell, Dave (1997) *Football and the English: A Social History of Association Football in England, 1863-1995*, Preston, Carnegie Publishing Ltd

Scottish Athletic Journal (1885) 'Modern Athletic Celebrities, Mr Andrew Watson' Glasgow, 15 December

Seddon, Peter (1999) *Steve Bloomer, The Story of Football's First Superstar*, Derby, The Breedon Books Publishing Company

Shyllon, Folarin (1977) *Black People in Britain 1555-1833*, Oxford University Press

Stuart, Ossie (1995) 'The Lions Stir: Football in African Society in Wagg, Stephen eds. *Giving the Game Away: Football, Politics and Culture on Five Continents*, London and New York, Leicester University Press,

Talburt, Tony (2012) *History on the Page: Adventures in Black British History*, London, New Generation Publishers

Taylor, Matthew (2008) *The Association Game, A History of British Football*, London, Pearson Longman

Taylor, Rose; Kafel, Andrew and Smith, Russell, (2006) *Images of England: Crossley Heath School*, Gloucestershire, Tempus Publishing Limited

Thomas, C.Y. (1988) *The Poor and the Powerless: Economic Policy and Change in the Caribbean*, London, Latin America Bureau

Thomas, W.E.S. (1985) 'Revolution, Romanticism and Victorianism' in Haigh, Christopher eds. *The Cambridge Historical Encyclopedia of Great Britain and Ireland*, Cambridge University Press

UCL, 2016, Legacies of British Slave Ownership, Https://www.ucl.ac.uk/lbs accessed on 12 July 2015

Vamplew, Wray (1988) 'Sport and Industrialisation: An Economic Interpretation of the Changes in Popular Sport in Nineteenth Century England' in Mangan, J.A. eds. *Pleasure, Profit and Proselytism, British Culture and Sport at Home and Abroad 1700-1914*, London, Frank Cass

Vasili, Phil (1998) *The First Black Footballer: Arthur Wharton 1865-1930*, London, Frank Cass Publishers

Vasili, Philip (2000) *Colouring Over the White Line: The History of Black Footballers in Britain*, Edinburgh and London, Mainstream Publishing Company

Walvin, James (1973) *Black and White: The Negro and English Society 1555-1945*, London, Allen Lane The Penguin Press

Walvin, James (1994a) 'Black People in Britain' in Tibbles, Anthony eds. *Transatlantic Slavery Against Human Dignity*, London, HMSO

Walvin, James (1994b) *The People's Game: The History of Football Revisited*, Edinburgh and London, Mainstream Publishing Company

Warsop, Keith (2004) *The Early FA Cup Finals and the Southern Amateurs*, Nottingham, SoccaData Publishing

West, Shearer (1996) *The Victorians and Race*, Aldershot, Brookfield USA, Ashgate Publishers